# SEARCHING BEYOND THE STARS

## SEVEN WOMEN IN SCIENCE TAKE ON SPACE'S BIGGEST QUESTIONS

WRITTEN BY
**NICOLE MORTILLARO**

ILLUSTRATED BY
**AMANDA KEY**

annick press
toronto · berkeley

For all the women who have been told they couldn't or shouldn't,
and for my daughter Sara: "Never cruel or cowardly.
Never give up, never give in."
—N.M.

For my family.
—A.K.

Cover art by Amanda Key, designed by Paul Covello
Interior designed by Paul Covello and Sara Loos
Edited by Katie Hearn and Kaela Cadieux
Line edited by Doeun Rivendell
Copy edited by Mary Ann Blair
Proofread by Doeun Rivendell

Annick Press Ltd.

We acknowledge the support of the Canada Council for the Arts and the Ontario Arts Council, and the participation of
the Government of Canada/la participation du gouvernement du Canada for our publishing activities.

Library and Archives Canada Cataloguing in Publication

Title: Searching beyond the stars : seven women in science take on space's biggest questions /
    written by Nicole Mortillaro ; illustrated by Amanda Key.
Names: Mortillaro, Nicole, 1972- author. | Key, Amanda, illustrator.
Description: Includes bibliographical references and index.
Identifiers: Canadiana (print) 20220171866 | Canadiana (ebook) 20220171882 | ISBN 9781773216256
    (hardcover) | ISBN 9781773216249 (softcover) | ISBN 9781773216270 (PDF) | ISBN 9781773216263
    (HTML)
Subjects: LCSH: Women astronomers—Biography—Juvenile literature. | LCSH: Women in astronomy—
    Juvenile literature. | LCSH: Space sciences—Juvenile literature. | LCGFT: Biographies.
Classification: LCC QB34.5 .M67 2022 | DDC j520.92/52—dc23

Published in the U.S.A. by Annick Press (U.S.) Ltd.
Distributed in Canada by University of Toronto Press.
Distributed in the U.S.A. by Publishers Group West.

Printed in China

annickpress.com
amandakey.design

Also available as an e-book. Please visit annickpress.com/ebooks for more details.

# TABLE OF CONTENTS

# OPENING UP THE UNIVERSE

When you think of a scientist, what image comes to mind? If you're like a lot of people, you might see a man in a lab coat or a man peering through a telescope. I know that was the case for me when I was growing up as I dreamed of heading to the stars. That's because, for the most part, that's all I saw: on TV, in the movies, and in the news.

As I got older, I realized that there are *so many* women who have contributed to what I love most: space and space exploration. But their stories were left untold as they stood in the shadows of men who were doing the same things they were.

Today, we are starting to recognize many more women for their remarkable contributions and achievements—women who are discovering new worlds, searching for alien signals, and unlocking the mysteries of the universe. So I wanted to highlight some of them in this book. Some did their research in the recent past, paving the way for others to continue breaking barriers and exploring exciting new frontiers of space research.

For this book, I was able to speak with Jill Tarter, who was at the forefront of the search for the first extraterrestrial intelligence; Sara Seager, who is searching for potentially habitable planets; and Ashley Walker, who is one of the first Black women in the field of astrochemistry and is looking at what chemical combinations might give rise to life. Emily Lakdawalla shared with me her passion for communicating the wonders of space to the public, Tanya Harrison bubbled with excitement about all the wonders on Mars, and Renée Hložek pondered about our universe's beginnings . . . and how it may end. I truly consider it an honor to have been able to speak to some of the women I had read about and learned so much from, especially as a science communicator. Their enthusiasm is infectious. We all share an intense curiosity and a common passion: the love of the universe in which we live.

These incredible women are opening the entire universe up to us. They are looking back in time to the Big Bang, when everything we know and see came into existence; they are looking for planets that may harbor life or that may be good places to at least *start searching* for signs of life; and they are looking back at Mars to a time when it may have once had an ocean. Most of all, they are trying to learn what all of this means for humans.

I want anyone who reads this book to know that nothing can stop you from pursuing your dream, despite the challenges that you may need to overcome. Anyone who has a curious mind, who seeks answers to the tough, nagging questions—Where do we come from? How did life arise on Earth? What happened to the water on Mars? How will the universe end?—can try to get the answers.

So dip in and meet these women. See how they're all searching beyond the stars every day and how you might one day, too.

# NAVIGATING THIS BOOK

Want to learn more about the science and the history behind these scientists' awesome achievements? Or maybe you'd like to read some of the strangest space facts out there? Look for these sidebars throughout the book:

**A LITTLE BIT OF HISTORY**
The sidebars with this icon give context for each scientist's work and life—whether that's talking about the findings that paved the way for their own discoveries or the social realities that impacted the way their careers took shape.

**BEHIND THE SCIENCE**
From physics to chemistry to geology and beyond, these sidebars give insight into the factors that influenced the scientists' methods and approaches.

**SPACE ODDITY**
Space science is full of out-there attempts and unusual phenomena—just look to these sidebars for proof!

**DEFINITION**

Words in **bold** are further defined in the glossary at the back of the book.

# LEADING THE RACE

## KATHERINE JOHNSON TAKES US INTO ORBIT

# AN EYE FROM ABOVE

It's October 4, 1957.

Across the world, people crane their heads upward, searching for a faint light crossing the sky among the stars. It's not a comet or an asteroid—it's Sputnik, the first artificial satellite to be launched into space. Many people look on in fear as the beachball-sized satellite—built by the Union of Soviet Socialist Republics (U.S.S.R.), also known as the Soviet Union—looks down on them.

The U.S.S.R. is considered a powerful enemy to the United States, and Americans fear that this launch could usher in a new type of warfare. Were the Soviets using Sputnik to monitor their every move?

Katherine Goble is one of the people silently tracking the steadily moving dot across the night sky. But Katherine doesn't feel afraid. For her, it is the dawn of a new age—the Space Age.

# KATHERINE'S TIMELINE

**1939**
Becomes one of the first African American students to enroll at West Virginia State

**1918**
Born Katherine Coleman in White Sulphur Springs, West Virginia, USA

**1960**
Coauthors paper on calculations for getting a spacecraft into orbit

## 1962

Helps confirm calculations for the spaceflight for John Glenn, the first American to orbit Earth

## 1961

Calculates suborbital path for Alan Shepard, the first American astronaut in space

## 2015

Awarded the U.S. Presidential Medal of Freedom

# YOU NEED TO KNOW

### ARTIFICIAL SATELLITE

A human-made object that orbits Earth

### PROJECT MERCURY

The first U.S. human space program, created on October 7, 1958, and made up of seven astronauts

### APOLLO PROGRAM

The U.S. program, which ran from 1961 to 1975, that sent humans to the moon

# THE FIGHT FOR FLIGHT

When World War II ended in 1945, a new conflict began between the United States and the **U.S.S.R.**, two superpower countries that had both fought against Germany. The U.S.S.R. was afraid that Germany would be able to regain power. To prevent this from happening, they installed Communist governments like their own across Eastern Europe. As the United States watched this unfold, they began to worry about just how much control the U.S.S.R. was starting to hold.

This was the start of the Cold War—a race for superiority and dominance. Instead of fighting on battle-fields, both countries began to stockpile weapons, build stronger armies, and work on advanced technologies.

### THE U.S.S.R.

Known today as Russia, the Union of Soviet Socialist Republics was a former federal socialist state in northern Eurasia that existed from 1922 to 1991.

It was clear that the U.S. National Advisory Committee for Aeronautics (NACA) had to expand their focus to study the potential of spaceflight. The U.S.S.R. had already set their sights on getting to space, and this only ramped up the fear in the Western world. If the Soviets took hold of space, would they be able to rain bombs down on other countries?

The United States began by working on supersonic flight—planes that could go faster than the **speed of sound**. And they beat the U.S.S.R.: on October 14, 1947, U.S. army captain Chuck Yeager broke the speed of sound, also called the sound barrier, in the Bell X-1. America was ahead—at least until the launch of Sputnik.

### SPEED OF SOUND

The distance that a sound wave travels per unit of time. This differs depending on the material that the sound travels through—when traveling through air at 20°C (68°F), its speed is around 343 meters per second or 1,125 feet per second (1,235 kilometers per hour or 767 miles per hour).

As this new technological warfare was being developed, Katherine was working as a schoolteacher. She had always been fascinated with numbers. As a child, she would count anything she could, from forks and knives while doing dishes to the steps it would take her to walk to church. But at the time, being of African American descent meant that she wouldn't get the type of quality education white students would.

But her father recognized how bright she was, and he sent her to the best schools available to Black students. She skipped a couple of grades and eventually enrolled in a high school that was on the West Virginia State University campus, becoming one of just three Black students. She breezed through that, too, graduating when she was just 14. At 18, she started attending the university and eventually got a job teaching math.

" THE WHOLE IDEA OF GOING INTO SPACE WAS NEW AND DARING. THERE WERE NO TEXTBOOKS, SO WE HAD TO WRITE THEM. "

## NASA/NACA

The National Advisory Committee for Aeronautics (NACA) was formed by the United States in 1915 to study flight. It was renamed the National Aeronautics and Space Administration (NASA) in 1958 when their research focus expanded to include satellite and spaceflight programs.

That all changed in 1952, when she was alerted to a job at **NACA** at the Langley Research Center in Hampton, West Virginia. The committee was looking for "computers"—people, mostly women, who would conduct complex mathematical calculations for flight.

The idea of being a mathematician—and one who was serving her country in one of the most ambitious programs around—appealed to her greatly. And Katherine got the job.

Though she was well qualified, Katherine was still working in a highly segregated time when there was a definite division between Black people and white people across all areas of society. At NACA, the West Area Computers were made up of Black women, and the East Area Computers were made up of white women. Even bathrooms were divided by race.

No matter how smart Katherine proved herself to be, most white people—including some of her colleagues—viewed her as inferior simply because of her race. But Katherine didn't let it get to her. She simply concentrated on her work, and that work meant breaking new scientific barriers.

# THE HUMAN SPACE RACE

On January 31, 1958—four months after Sputnik was launched—the Americans had their own satellite, Explorer 1, in orbit around Earth.

What next? The Americans wanted to beat the Soviets at achieving human spaceflight. Flying a plane was one thing. So was sending an object into orbit around Earth. But sending a human being? There was far more at stake, and Katherine wanted to help.

Though the division between the East and West Computing facilities was finally dissolved in 1958, Katherine was still a woman, and a Black woman at that—and women weren't allowed to attend official meetings. When she asked why she couldn't attend, her supervisors didn't have a real explanation—they just said it wasn't something that was done. Rather than giving up, Katherine remained persistent, and later that year, she became the first woman to attend scientific briefings that discussed research findings. Instead of having to chase down information, she now had access to all the knowledge her male coworkers had. Shortly afterward, she also became the first woman in the division to author a report. For her, this fight wasn't about being Black or a woman. It was about having the access she needed to do her job right.

## RACISM IN AMERICA

After World War II, there was a push for equality for Black people, who had long been persecuted and discriminated against due to the violent legacy of slavery in America. In some parts of the country, Black people were forbidden from eating at restaurants or using the same water fountains as white people, and they were forced to ride at the back of buses. These rules have changed, but the fight for equality continues to this day.

As NASA worked hard to get the first man into space—under the mounting tension of the Cold War—Katherine pored over complicated calculations. She checked and rechecked her math. The first American trip into space would be **suborbital**, meaning the spacecraft would not complete an entire orbit around Earth. An **orbital flight** would be even more complicated, and it was NASA's eventual goal to get there.

It was planned for the spacecraft to splash down into the ocean. That meant additional rocket fuel wouldn't be needed to slow it down and the water would provide a natural cushion for the **astronaut** after his parachute deployed. Katherine was under enormous pressure to calculate the **trajectory** for the spacecraft—where it would go and where it would land.

There was so much riding on this flight. Calculations that were off even by a little bit could lead to tragedy: the rocket could come crashing down to Earth or drift off into space. Either way, the astronaut wouldn't survive. Though the stakes were incredibly high, NASA had faith in their "computers."

### COSMONAUT VS. ASTRONAUT

Cosmonauts are trained and certified by the Russian Space Agency to work in space, while astronauts are trained and certified by NASA or by the European Space Agency (ESA), the Canadian Space Agency (CSA), or the Japanese Aerospace Exploration Agency (JAXA).

But even Katherine's most brilliant work couldn't save NASA and the United States from yet another devastating defeat in the space race. On April 12, 1961, the world once again looked up in awe as Soviet **cosmonaut** Yuri Gagarin became the first human in space. The American spirit was crushed, and the nation's fear and doubt in the midst of the Cold War took an even deeper hold. Everyone at Langley took it hard, but while Katherine was disappointed, she knew that America wasn't actually that far behind. They may have not been the first, but they would find a way to make their mark in the space race—she would make sure of it.

KATHERINE JOHNSON - 15

# CALCULATED SUCCESS

The engineers and scientists at NASA doubled their efforts. In their rush to try to get into space, they tested rockets that exploded, didn't launch, or suffered other catastrophic malfunctions. All the while, Katherine's head was deep into calculations.

To her, getting a human into space was simple geometry. It was sort of like throwing a ball: it moves in an arc, or a parabola. Katherine was purported to say: "You tell me when you want it and where you want it to land, and I'll do it backwards and tell you when to take off." Finally, after weeks of intense effort, Katherine's work paid off. On May 5, 1961, the first U.S. astronaut, Alan Shepard, was ready to take flight on board a Mercury-Redstone rocket. But even as everyone at NASA prepared for launch, there were still lingering doubts. So many other rockets before this one had exploded. Were they rushing this launch just to try to catch up to the Soviets? Was it worth it with a life hanging in the balance?

## THE FORCES BEHIND FLIGHT

The science of flight is called aerodynamics. There are four forces of flight: lift, weight, thrust, and drag. A plane's wings provide lift to hold it in the air, but its weight pushes it down toward Earth. As the plane flies, drag from the air slows it down, which it overcomes with thrust, or forward movement, by using its engines. If any of these forces are disrupted, the plane can crash, which is why planes are fitted with ultrasensitive instruments.

While we take human spaceflight for granted today, with hundreds of people having successfully made the perilous voyage, Shepard would be only the second person to strap himself into a rocket, with a controlled explosion hurtling him off toward the stars. Millions of Americans—and millions more across the world—sat around their television sets, holding their collective breath.

The rocket blasted to life, the thunderous noise echoing across the Florida landscape. All eyes turned skyward as the black-and-white missile lifted into the blue sky and eventually disappeared out of sight. For more than 15 minutes, everyone watching at home and at Langley waited in suspense. Now that the United States had sent a human into space, the question remained: Would he survive, or had they just witnessed a man rocketing to his death?

Finally, word arrived: Shepard had splashed down safely in the Atlantic Ocean. He had reached a breakneck speed of 8,336 kilometers per hour (5,180 miles per hour) and a height of 187 kilometers (116 miles) in his short trip. America had finally gotten to space. Now that they'd done it once, they had renewed confidence that they could continue to do it. Katherine's work had barely started.

NASA's next goal was orbital spaceflight. The launch was scheduled for February 20, 1962, with the intention of having astronaut John Glenn complete seven full orbits. This was a whole new type of launch—including a new Atlas rocket—and landing, and Katherine knew it.

Glenn had faith in NASA—you'd have to in order to agree to sit atop a 260,000-pound (130-ton) rocket full of fuel that could explode at any time—but as with any good pilot, he wanted to review the numbers ahead of his launch. They had been generated by an IBM computer, relatively new to the organization, but he wanted to be sure the calculations were correct.

"Get the girl to check the numbers," he said. He meant Katherine.

Katherine worked diligently for almost two days to ensure the numbers were correct. She went over different scenarios, accounting for any kind of situation. In the end, the numbers matched. Though Glenn had to cut short his planned seven orbits due to a problem with the capsule, he landed just 64 kilometers (40 miles) off-course after 4 hours and 56 minutes in orbit around Earth. The difference in landing location wasn't a result of any miscalculation; it was because of the unexpected weight of more fuel on board.

The mission was deemed a success. It was clear that Katherine was just as precise and reliable as the IBM computer, and her work gave Glenn the assurance needed to make this remarkable spaceflight possible.

# TO THE MOON

More missions followed Glenn's, all of them successful. Meanwhile, the Soviets also continued to launch more of their cosmonauts. Now, the United States decided to go one giant leap further: to the moon. If they could pull this off, they would prove their technical might to the Soviet Union on the world stage—once and for all. On September 12, 1962, President John F. Kennedy issued a bold statement: Americans would land on the moon before the end of the decade.

NASA had a daring task ahead of them. For one, they would need a rocket far bigger than any they had. And landing a rocket on the moon while the moon also moved through space would require extensive and extremely precise calculations. The margin for error would be even smaller than with Glenn's orbital flight. Tens of thousands of people worked on the program—engineers, scientists, computers, and technicians. By this time, Katherine had joined NASA's Space Mechanics Division and computed backup navigational charts for the missions in case the electronics failed.

Eventually, the scientists and engineers devised a spacecraft that would be like no other: it would consist of two separate parts—the command module and the lunar lander—that would be joined together for the trip to the moon. Then, once at their destination, the two parts would separate, with the lander heading to the moon with two of the astronauts on board. One astronaut would stay in the command module, which would remain in orbit. There was one essential question left to answer: How would NASA get those two astronauts to rendezvous with the orbiter?

It required complex geometry and calculating the speed and movement of both the lander and the moon itself—and Katherine worked with the team to get those answers. It was in part due to her incredible skill as a mathematician that the men of Apollo 11 made history as the first humans to walk on another world: our moon.

## THE MOON

How did the moon come to be? Astronomers still don't know for certain, but the most popular theory is that at some point in our solar system's formation, a giant body—perhaps the size of Mars—smashed into our newly forming planet. The debris left over from the impact circled our planet and finally came together, forming our planet's closest companion.

# . . . AND BEYOND

Katherine retired from NASA in 1986. During her time at the organization, she had broken through incredible barriers, both as a Black woman and as a scientist. But her lifelong contributions remained unknown to many until 2015, when Katherine was given the Presidential Medal of Freedom by President Barack Obama.

In 2016, Margot Lee Shetterly wrote a book, *Hidden Figures*, on the contributions of the Black women mathematicians at NASA. It was made into a movie of the same name, which gained critical praise for finally bringing the Black women of NASA out of the shadows. After the success of the movie, 98-year-old Katherine was finally rocketed to well-deserved recognition. She was honored by NASA and remained in the spotlight for months.

Katherine died on February 24, 2020, but her work continues to help pave the way for further moon missions. NASA has a bold plan to return to the moon with its Artemis mission, which will see the first woman land on our dusty, rocky neighbor. Her historical arrival on the lunar surface will be thanks, in part, to Katherine—the woman who first got us to the moon.

# EARS ON THE SKY

## JILL TARTER
## LISTENS FOR ALIEN TECHNOLOGIES

# IS ANYBODY OUT THERE?

The search for intelligent extraterrestrial life started more than 60 years ago, during the dawn of the **Space Age**, when humans first began to leave the confines of Earth. At the time, our understanding of the universe beyond Earth was changing drastically. We were beginning to understand that among the billions of galaxies and stars were potentially billions of other worlds. We were sending satellites into orbit around Earth and beginning to send human beings into space. Our spacecraft—ambassadors of Earth—were visiting far-off planets in our solar system.

Jill Tarter spent 30 years searching for aliens, poring through data collected from some of the world's most sophisticated telescopes to listen for a message and heading some of the most detailed searches ever undertaken. Thanks to her work, we are inching ever closer to answering a fundamental question that humanity has asked ever since we first looked up at the stars: Are we alone?

# JILL'S TIMELINE

**1984**

Helps cofound the SETI Institute

**1944**

Born Jill Cornell in Tuckahoe, New York, USA

**1989**

Awarded a Lifetime Achievement Award from Women in Aerospace

## 2002

Elected a Fellow of the American Association for the Advancement of Science

## 2004

Named one of the 100 most influential people in the world by *Time* magazine

## 2009

Received a 2009 TED Prize

# YOU NEED TO KNOW

## GALAXY

A massive collection of stars, gas, and dust bound together by gravity. Our galaxy is called the Milky Way.

## SETI

The search for extraterrestrial intelligence. The SETI Institute was founded with the goal of finding intelligent alien life in our galaxy.

## RADIO TELESCOPE

Unlike an optical telescope, which sees stars visually—just like our eyes do—a radio telescope "listens" to radio waves. These telescopes look like giant satellite dishes.

## ELECTROMAGNETIC RADIATION

Waves of light and energy move around us, including microwaves, infrared, visible light, ultraviolet, X-rays, gamma rays, and radio waves. Radio signals leave Earth and travel at the speed of light (300,000 kilometers per second or 186,000 miles per second) into space.

## RADIO FREQUENCIES

A frequency is the number of waves that pass a particular point every second. In the search for a signal from other intelligent life, astronomers look over a range of radio and optical frequencies searching for patterns that aren't produced by natural objects like stars or black holes.

# SCANNING THE SKIES FOR SIGNALS

So how exactly do we find other existing civilizations? Jill's decades-long search didn't involve looking through telescopes the way you might think, watching twinkling stars in the dark. Her telescopes were giant dishes that were still aimed at the stars—but they were listening. Specifically, they were listening for radio transmissions from worlds that might be orbiting these stars, much in the same way you listen to a radio station in a car.

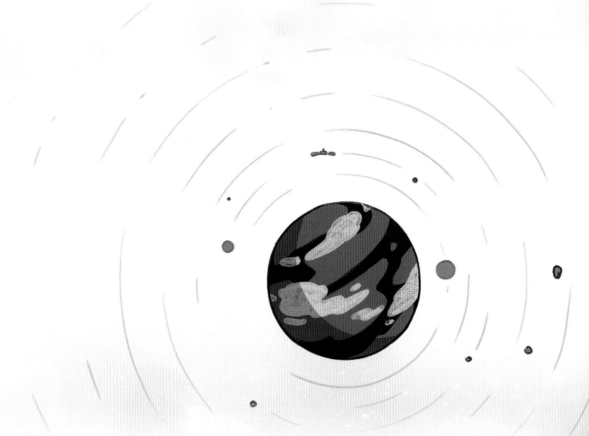

Radio waves come from many natural sources. In the universe, stars, galaxies, **nebulae** (clouds of gas), and other objects emit radio waves across varying frequencies. So how can astronomers tell if a radio signal is coming from a natural source or an alien civilization?

In 1959, the scientific journal *Nature* published the article "Searching for Interstellar Communications." The authors surmised that alien civilizations might use radio communication just as we do; these signals would extend into space and be distinct from ones emitted naturally by celestial bodies. Celestial bodies give off radio signals that cover a range of frequencies, while technologies made by humans produce radio signals that occur at unique, single frequencies.

Just think about life here on Earth. We use radio signals to listen to music, watch TV, and communicate. Those signals, though weak, travel outward from our planet. If they were stronger, they could travel vast distances across space. And if they were pointed in a particular direction, they could end up being intercepted by someone else—an alien civilization.

### THE ARECIBO MESSAGE

In 1974, humans sent the most powerful radio signal ever out into space toward a cluster of stars called Messier 13 using the Arecibo radio telescope in Puerto Rico. Their goal was to show how powerful the transmitter was, but it was the first real attempt to send out a signal like this to any potential alien civilization that might be in that area. So far there hasn't been a response—but that's because it will take more than 21,000 years to reach the star system. But who knows? Someone might intercept it along the way!

Similarly, the authors suggested that we might be able to hear aliens by scanning the skies on particular radio frequencies. In fact, some astronomers believe that some of these alien civilizations may even be directing a signal outward into space to see if anyone is listening. And we are. Just like we send out radio signals, we can also receive them using large radio telescopes. The authors concluded that "the probability of success is difficult to estimate, but if we never search, the chance of success is zero." That's why astronomers keep their ears pointed toward the stars.

## THE DRAKE EQUATION

Do you like math? How's this for a mathematical equation: $N = Rf_p n_e f_l f_i f_c L$.

This is the Drake Equation—devised by Frank Drake—a formula that estimates the number of technologically advanced civilizations that might exist in our galaxy.

In this equation:

- $N$ is the number of detectable civilizations in our galaxy.
- $R$ is the rate of star formation in the galaxy.
- $f_p$ is the fraction of stars that form planets.
- $n_e$ is the number of planets with an environment that can support life (i.e., Earth-like planets).
- $f_l$ is the fraction of these planets on which life actually emerges.
- $f_i$ is the fraction of these planets on which intelligent life arises.
- $f_c$ is the fraction of these civilizations that are capable of interstellar communication.
- $L$ is the length of time such a civilization remains detectable.

So what's the answer? It's hard to say. This is because estimates for the value of $N$ range from one to several million. But even if the equation doesn't have a solution, it's still helpful when discussing the likelihood of extraterrestrial intelligence.

In 1960, the **astrophysicist** Frank Drake used a radio telescope in Green Bank, West Virginia, to conduct the very first search for extraterrestrial signals. Called OZMA, the project operated for two months, searching a very specific radio band while observing two nearby stars.

## ASTROPHYSICIST

A scientist who studies how the universe works

"
DO WHATEVER IT IS YOU LOVE DOING. BUT MAKE SURE YOU GET VERY, VERY GOOD AT SOME SKILL; BECOME AN EXPERT. THEN WHEN THINGS CHANGE IN THE FUTURE, YOU CAN FIGURE OUT HOW TO USE YOUR SKILLS TO THRIVE IN THAT CHANGED ENVIRONMENT.
"

There was some excitement when the telescope picked up a signal. Unfortunately, it was later discovered that it had come from a nearby spy plane. Still, that ground-breaking experiment—the first **SETI** search in history—was an important lesson in how to refine the search over radio frequencies. Though Jill didn't know it, she would draw on that study in her own work years later.

# JILL'S SPECIAL LANGUAGE

Growing up in the 1940s and '50s, Jill never fit the stereotypical image of a young girl. She loved fishing, hunting, and the great outdoors, always encouraged by her father. They would take long walks on the beach together at night, in Manasota Key, Florida. It was there that Jill, looking up in awe at the velvet curtain of black sky punctured by millions of tiny lights, discovered her lifelong curiosity about the universe.

After high school, she applied for a bloodline scholarship to Cornell University (it turned out she was related to its founder, Ezra Cornell) to study engineering but was denied because it was reserved for men only. But she soon received an offer from the consumer goods company Procter & Gamble, which offered to pay her five-year scholarship. Jill was the only woman in the university's engineering program.

Jill excelled at Cornell, earning a degree in engineering physics. But engineering bored her. Frank Drake's search for extraterrestrial signals years before had inspired a new interest in the field—NASA, too, had briefly searched for signals in the 1960s and '70s. Independent astronomers were also at work, and a new branch of radio astronomy

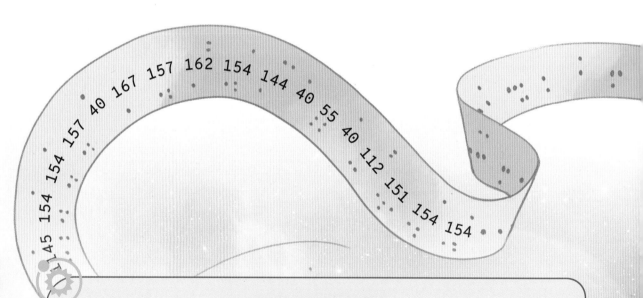

## IN LOCO PARENTIS

When Jill was at Cornell, the university had a policy termed *in loco parentis*, Latin for "in the place of parents." The university felt it was legally responsible for the safety of the students. Under this policy, female students were locked in their rooms from 10 p.m. to 6 a.m. as a way of "protecting" them. So, in the evenings, while the men were allowed to study and solve problems together and share knowledge, Jill was forced to make it on her own.

had taken hold. Jill wanted to be a part of that. Now married with a child, she moved with her family to California to study astronomy at the University of California, Berkeley.

There she met astronomer Stu Bowyer, who had been given an old computer to use in his research. The only problem was that it had no high-level programming language, and Stu wasn't an expert in dealing with such a machine. But Jill was. She had learned the Octal computer language while completing her master's degree, working on a PDP-8/S, a revolutionary computer that was small enough to fit on a desk—something highly unusual for the time. While most computers communicate using binary code, or the base-2 number system (just two digits: 0 and 1), Octal uses the base-8 system, or numbers 0 to 7. The PDP-8/S could do 11 different operations depending on what Octal code was written.

Stu approached Jill about collaborating on a new field of study, the search for extraterrestrial intelligence—her experience was a perfect fit. He gave her a copy of a recently published report called *Project Cyclops*, now often referred to as the "Bible of SETI." Its groundbreaking ideas outlined why and how humanity should be seeking out signals from other intelligent life.

Jill knew about the SETI program, and it intrigued her. Now, she would seek to answer the question of whether we were alone in the universe by turning to the same velvet sky she'd looked up at with her father, but this time she would use powerful scientific tools to listen for voices in the darkness.

## THE FERMI PARADOX

Astrophysicist Enrico Fermi once wondered, "Where are all the aliens?" His idea was that an alien civilization with rocket technology should be able to colonize the galaxy within tens to hundreds of million years. Our galaxy is roughly 13 billion years old. So where are the aliens? We still don't know.

# REFINING SIGNALS AND ADVANCING THE SEARCH

Jill finished her PhD and volunteered for SETI research, working with Stu on SERENDIP—the Search for Extraterrestrial Radio Emissions from Nearby Developed Intelligent Populations—a program at the University of California, Berkeley.

Instead of booking time on large radio telescopes to specifically look for signals, SERENDIP used the observations and data from telescopes that other astronomers were using to look at different things in what is called a "piggyback" observation. It then analyzed this data. It never did find a voice in the dark, but different, updated versions of the search continued.

## HOW DO YOU LISTEN?

There are a couple of ways to use radio telescopes to search for alien signals. One is a direct approach, where a telescope is pointed at a particular target, like a star that is believed to have a planet in orbit. Another is a wider search, where radio telescopes scan large parts of the sky.

In 1984, Jill cofounded the SETI Institute along with Tom Pierson, an administrator from San Francisco State University. Here, a dedicated group of astronomers used telescopes to search for alien signals. This meant that instead of searching intermittently for potential signals from an intelligent civilization, astronomers could look for them on a regular basis, as long as they could raise funds from government sources and private donors.

One of Jill's biggest projects at the Institute was directing Project Phoenix. Beginning in 1995, Jill spent almost 10 years leading the search for signals from more than 800 nearby stars using telescopes from around the world, which was entirely funded through private donations. These telescopes searched narrowband frequencies and were able to process the data quickly and do a follow-up with any potential star systems that might have intelligent life capable of sending a signal, which involved using two telescopes at two separate locations. This eliminated any chance that a signal detected could be local, meaning coming from Earth. The project was also uniquely able to eliminate human-caused, terrestrial signals that might be misinterpreted. Though no alien signals were detected, it was the largest attempt ever undertaken.

In part because of Jill's work, SETI research was starting to be seen as more widely acceptable, even valuable. But the Institute still didn't have its own telescopes; Jill and her colleagues had to book time on telescopes elsewhere when they were available, and this slowed them down. They determined that building their own telescope would cost a whopping $25 million—an incredibly difficult amount of money to raise for something that might never see a return on investment.

Jill contacted Paul Allen, the cofounder of Microsoft, who had donated funds for her research on Project Phoenix. She hoped he would be interested in donating more. He was, and in 2007, the Allen Telescope Array (ATA) officially became operational. It had a total of 42 dishes of the originally planned 350, each 6.1 meters (20 feet) across. The ATA sped up the SETI search by a factor of 100. Instead of being able to search approximately 1,000 stars over 20 years, it could search up to a million or more.

Project Phoenix was vitally important to advancing the search for extraterrestrial signals. Sure, you could point radio telescopes at stars and listen on a particular frequency, but there's a right way and a wrong way. And the wrong way is doing it intermittently. The ATA provided the dedicated group of telescopes needed to do the job right.

## SETI@HOME

In 1999, the UC Berkeley SETI program launched the SETI@home project, where home computers could run a free program that would analyze data collected by the Arecibo radio telescope. The program paused in 2020, after astronomers said they had analyzed all the data they could and would focus on studying the results.

In 2000, Jill became the director of the Center of SETI Research at the Institute, later called the Carl Sagan Center for Research. Just two years later, Jill and her colleague Margaret Turnbull were behind another important advancement for SETI. They created HabCat, a catalog of star systems that could potentially be home to habitable worlds. The implications were huge: HabCat refined the search for signals down from nearly 250 billion stars in the Milky Way to a much more precise list. It included 17,129 stars that could potentially contain habitable planets capable of hosting complex life.

# ONWARD AND UPWARD

Jill's hard work and determination earned her many distinctions. She received the Lifetime Achievement Award from Women in Aerospace in 1989 and two public service medals from NASA. She was named one of the 100 most influential people in the world by *Time* magazine in 2004. In 2009, she received the TED Prize, given to those who are working to make a global change.

Jill was also the inspiration for the character of Ellie Arroway in the book *Contact* by renowned astronomer Carl Sagan, which was later made into a blockbuster Hollywood movie. Though fictional, it helped bring to the public eye the real search for extraterrestrial signals.

After stepping down as the director of the Center for SETI Research in 2012, Jill focused on funding SETI research, approaching private donors and speaking at conferences worldwide. Her successes in securing that funding show just how much this new frontier in space science has captured the public's imagination.

When Jill started her career, it was thought that some stars might hold planets. Now, almost 30 years after the first **exoplanet**—a planet outside of our solar system—was discovered, we know that almost all stars are home to a planet, or even several, greatly expanding Jill's field for research. Today, radio telescopes are more sensitive, and computers can verify data that astronomers in the past would have had to check themselves. Jill had a hand in helping improve these technologies and methods, and that work will help astronomers carry on her search for generations to come.

While Jill may not have made alien contact, she hasn't given up hope that we will one day receive that historic radio transmission—one that will have traversed the vast distances in our galaxy to let us know that we aren't alone and that humanity wasn't some freak cosmic accident. In her 2009 TED Talk in Long Beach, California, after winning the TED Prize, Jill summed up the future of SETI: "I wish that you would empower Earthlings everywhere to become active participants in the ultimate search for cosmic company."

Who knows? One day soon, we may detect a signal that says, "You are *not* alone."

# TALKING SPACE

## EMILY LAKDAWALLA BRINGS SCIENCE TO THE PEOPLE

**?**

Is the second stage also on earth-escape trajectory or will it fall into the ocean somewhere?

**Emily Lakdawalla** @elakdawalla

Good question! The answer is that the upper stage is always also on an interplanetary trajectory! Every interplanetary mission has been followed into deep space by a dead rocket.

**Emily Lakdawalla** @elakdawalla

For some context, 50km is biggish for an asteroid, but still way too small to be round. The smallest solar system worlds that are round are closer to 400km in diameter, but those are icy. Only one rock world is sphereish: the biggest asteroid, Ceres.

# THE SPACE EVANGELIST

Emily Lakdawalla loves space. She loves the rings and many moons of Saturn; the colorful, swirling storm clouds on Jupiter; and the dusty, rock-strewn landscape of Mars. She is fascinated with the solar system and our place in it.

It's that passion, and her desire to share it with the world, that landed her a job at The Planetary Society, where she brings the wonder of space and our role in it to a whole new generation. Emily used to call herself the Space Evangelist, but now refers to herself as a space specialist. No matter what her latest Twitter handle is, though, her mission is clear: to spread the word about space to her nearly 200,000 online followers and beyond.

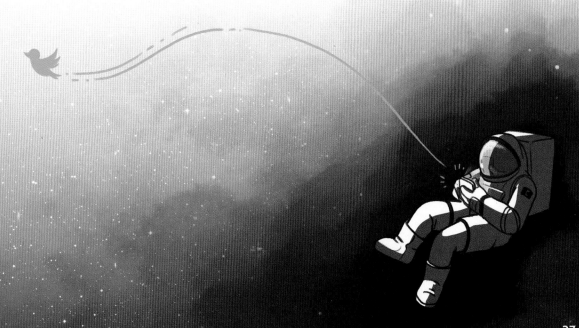

# EMILY'S TIMELINE

**2011**

Is awarded the Jonathan Eberhart Planetary Sciences Journalism Award for her article about a ring around Saturn

**2002**

Writes her first blog for The Planetary Society

**1975**

Born in Williamstown, Massachusetts, USA

## 2014

Has an asteroid named after her by the International Astronomical Union

## 2017

Receives an honorary doctorate from the Open University

## 2020

Leaves The Planetary Society

# YOU NEED TO KNOW

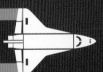

### THE PLANETARY SOCIETY

Founded by famed cosmologists (scientists who study the universe) Carl Sagan, Bruce Murray, and Louis Friedman in 1980 to promote space exploration. Today, the Society boasts more than 5,000 members in more than 100 countries.

### ROVERS

Machines that move around the surface of a planet or moon, kind of like a small car. We've sent many rovers to Mars, including Opportunity, Spirit, Curiosity and, most recently, Perseverance.

### SATELLITE

An object that orbits something else in space. It can be something natural, like the moon, or human-made, like the machines that provide us with satellite television by transmitting signals sent from Earth back down into our homes.

# SHARING SPACE

*"Just imagine this scene. You're on Mars, in Gale crater, with Curiosity. The sun has just set, and the temperature is falling rapidly. You look up. You see brilliant, wispy clouds, still sunlit even though night has fallen where you're standing. They're high in elevation, so the Sun can still reach them. As you stand there, skygazing, feeling increasingly chilled, the noctilucent clouds waft along in the Martian air, dimming from east to west as the Sun sets on them."*

This is how Emily describes the appearance of **noctilucent clouds**, a phenomenon of rare, high-altitude clouds that are luminous just after sunset or just before sunrise. They are found on Earth as well as Mars.

In this blog post on The Planetary Society's website, she's describing the view from Curiosity, a rover trundling across the surface of Mars (see page 60). Her vivid descriptions achieve the impossible, putting readers right on Mars with the rover, imagining the view that humans might one day see when they call Mars home.

Emily brings life to far-off worlds and distant landscapes, whether she's writing about findings on Mars; missions to asteroids that shed light on the birth of our solar system and how the building blocks of life might have been carried to Earth on these ancient rocks; or discoveries from a spacecraft flyby of Pluto, the icy world beyond our eighth planet, Neptune.

## PLUTO AND NEW HORIZON

Until August 2006, our solar system had nine planets: Mercury, Venus, Earth, Mars, Jupiter, Saturn, Uranus, Neptune, and Pluto. But that year, the International Astronomical Union decided that Pluto was no longer a planet. They classified it as a dwarf planet instead—a celestial body that orbits the sun, is round, and has other, smaller objects near it—comets, asteroids, or other dwarf planets. NASA launched a mission, New Horizons, to study it. The spacecraft was the fastest ever launched, traversing five billion kilometers (three billion miles) to provide us with the first-ever look at this peculiar world.

> **"YOU CAN LEARN WHEREVER YOU GO."**

Why does being an efficient science communicator matter?

We don't know how life began on Earth. We are still trying to understand how the ingredients of life may have been transported here through comets or asteroids. It's all about unraveling the mysteries of what makes us, well, us. Humans are explorers—we seek to learn. And Emily knows how to share that curiosity with her followers.

Who cares what a mission to an asteroid found? Why is any of that important? Emily takes all that complex information and explains how it relates back to us. Finding out what a comet looks like and how it came to be tells us about the early formation of the solar system and ultimately how Earth was originally created. It provides yet another clue into the processes that led to life—*human life*.

It may seem like this doesn't have any impact on day-to-day life, but that couldn't be further from the truth. Even if we aren't scientists ourselves, science impacts nearly every aspect of our lives, from laws and policies to the types of products available to us. When it comes to Emily's work, she's inspiring a sense of curiosity and helping us unlock the mystery of where we come from. The more we know, the better.

# FROM TEACHING ON EARTH TO LEARNING IN SPACE

Even before she became a science communicator, Emily spent a lot of time talking about science. She had gone to university to study **geology** and then went on to teach science at an elementary school.

## GEOLOGY AND PLANETARY GEOLOGY

Geology is the science of examining Earth's physical history, structure, and composition. Planetary geology studies the same things but for celestial bodies: planets, moons, asteroids, comets, and meteorites.

Though Emily had always been interested in space, the mission of the Mars Pathfinder really grabbed her attention. The spacecraft launched to Mars on December 4, 1996, and landed on July 4, 1997. The mission also had a rover, Sojourner, which slowly drove around the planet conducting scientific research, including studying the elements that make up the planet's rocky surface as well as its atmosphere and weather. It was an amazing first for Mars research, and it fascinated Emily.

At the same time, NASA's Galileo spacecraft was returning photographs from Jupiter, our solar system's largest planet. Emily marveled at the images she saw: its swirling clouds, including the Great Red Spot, a raging storm that's at least 400 years old; and Europa, a mysterious icy moon of the giant planet.

All of this deeply excited Emily. She was still working as a teacher at the time but found herself more and more amazed by how truly cool space is. The study of some planets and moons involved geology, which she had already studied. Could she actually make a career out of both geology and space? Emily was determined to find out—she left her teaching job to pursue a master's degree in planetary geology.

In 2001, The Planetary Society advertised a job that seemed made for her. It would involve her skills as a teacher and her education as a scientist. The Society was looking for a deputy project manager for their Red Rover Goes to Mars project, an education and public outreach program on the Mars Exploration Rover (MER) mission. The role would involve working with scientists and engineers at NASA's Jet Propulsion Laboratory, which is behind missions to Mars.

### MARS EXPLORATION ROVERS

NASA has sent two robotic ambassadors to Mars: Spirit and Opportunity. These two car-sized rovers, launched in 2003, were originally intended to last just 90 Martian days, but they went far, far longer. Spirit landed on January 4, 2004, and lasted until 2011. Opportunity lasted until 2018. Both rovers gathered data that showed Mars was once a watery world—something that could have enormous implications if we truly hope to live there one day.

Emily landed the job and was overjoyed. As project manager, she ran contests that chose high school students from around the world to work on training exercises for rover operations. After training, the students worked in actual MER operations, at the center of the action—from right where spacecraft on Mars were being sent driving instructions!

Once the contests were over, Emily remained on, starting a blog to write about The Planetary Society's ongoing role in space research. Her first post was about a Society-funded team, in conjunction with SETI (see page 33), that was sent to Devon Island in the Canadian high Arctic. The island is often used as an **analogue**, or a similar environment, for Mars. The team gathered data to study the potential of future airplanes that could one day be used on the Red Planet.

## THE ARCTIC MARS ANALOGUE

To train for Mars missions, both NASA and the European Space Agency have conducted many "missions" in the high Arctic. Why? It turns out parts of it are dry, rocky, and without vegetation, much like Mars itself, making it a great stand-in, or analogue, for the Red Planet.

In that post, she explained what created the Haughton Crater on Devon Island millions of years ago:

"A giant meteorite, perhaps 1 kilometer (0.6 mile) in diameter, plowed into the scene. It may have happened in the broad daylight of summer or in the bleak darkness of winter—we may never know. In either case, the impact, delivering an energy equivalent to 100 million kilotons of TNT, would have produced a blinding flash of light, then a monumental air blast that obliterated almost all life for several hundred kilometers around. A colossal shock wave expanded through the ground as the impactor dumped its cosmic momentum into the Earth, blending into the target rocks and vanishing as a superheated gas."

That was it. Emily was hooked on communicating about space to the public. She loved breaking down the science behind planets, discoveries, and space missions. Her previous experience as a teacher gave her the skills to explain difficult concepts and make them exciting. And people responded enthusiastically to her amazing ability to do so. Since her first post, Emily has gained almost 200,000 followers and posted more than 3,000 blog entries.

On top of that, she was the editor of The Planetary Society's member magazine, *The Planetary Report*, and contributed regularly to their weekly podcast, *Planetary Radio*. She shares amazing images from space and inspires discussion about what Mars might have looked like billions of years ago, for example, or how the ingredients for life could have been brought to Earth.

# TWITTERVERSE AND BEYOND

On any given day you can find Emily in her home office in front of three computer screens. On one screen might be a new research paper about a planetary mission. On another, it might be Twitter, where she's extremely active, communicating not only with the public but with other scientists. And on the third screen might be a draft of her latest article. Of course, that's when she's not busy traveling, talking at speaking engagements, or attending conferences.

Emily uses social media—mainly Twitter—to engage with her followers about exciting space news and developments in various missions. She stays away from YouTube, though, something she says many women in science do. Why's that? On Twitter, she can block abusive people, but comments about women science communicators can be much more aggressive on YouTube, and Emily's not willing to spend her time blocking insults and derogatory remarks.

Instead, she'd rather use her energy getting people excited about the latest space mission or discovery. What makes her most happy, in fact, is when her readers reach out to let her know they understand and when they get just as passionate as she does about what she's written. "Thank you for sharing!" and "Very cool!" are common responses to her tweets. Her followers often ask her questions, and she's always keen on replying. Her interaction with her audience is part of the reason Emily is so popular.

Because she is so passionate about her role as a science communicator, Emily has also written a book: *The Design and Engineering of Curiosity: How the Mars Rover Performs Its Job*. Reviewers have called her work "hard to put down" and "remarkable," another testament to Emily's ability to bring complicated science to the public.

## AN ASTEROID OF HER OWN

Asteroid 274860 was formally named "Emilylakdawalla" by the International Astronomical Union on July 12, 2014. The asteroid, left over from the early formation of our solar system, orbits the sun once every 5.14 years and was discovered in 2009.

Another one of her passions is using raw image data from the Juno spacecraft, in orbit around Jupiter, to create mind-blowing images of the swirling clouds of our biggest planet. The spacecraft is in orbit studying various aspects of Jupiter, but it's also equipped with a camera, called JunoCam. NASA has allowed public access to all the images it takes, encouraging the public to be creative in constructing beautiful photographs of their own and sharing them. This helps scientists determine what more they'd like to learn, and then they can plan where to take new photos.

## IMAGING

Imaging planets or other beautiful objects in our universe isn't as easy as simply taking a photograph. There's a lot of work behind the truly stunning pictures you may have seen of outer space—Saturn's rings, Jupiter's swirling storms, or far-off galaxies or nebulae (dark collections of gas and dust). Many telescopes and cameras on spacecraft don't take one single photo the way you might on a camera. Instead, they take several images that people put together using different filters, which can include colors and wavelengths that the human eye can't see. The images are combined to produce one final image, helping us see things that we might never have otherwise, such as details in the clouds.

# MORE TO SHARE

All of Emily's hard work hasn't gone unnoticed.

In 2011, she won the Jonathan Eberhart Planetary Sciences Journalism Award from the Division for Planetary Sciences of the American Astronomical Society for a blog entry about one of Saturn's rings, which is associated with a small moon, Phoebe. The article doesn't just talk about the scientific paper that revealed this new ring. Instead, Emily analyzes for readers all of Saturn's major rings, including explanations for some stunning photographs sent back by the Cassini spacecraft, which orbited Saturn from 2004 to 2017.

In September 2020, in her final blog post, "A Goodbye, but Not Forever, from Emily Lakdawalla," Emily announced that she was leaving The Planetary Society after 19 years. She said that she was taking some time to finish her second book but would continue as a contributing editor for the astronomy magazine *Sky & Telescope*.

"I am sure that whatever I do, it will involve translating and distilling highly technical information into stories and graphics that generate awe about what humans are doing and discovering in space," she wrote.

With spacecraft being sent out from all corners of the globe—from the United States to China, India, and Russia—space exploration is reaching new heights all the time. So there will likely be no shortage of stories for Emily to share. There are also new, private companies on the scene, including SpaceX and Blue Origin, which are taking space travel from the government level to the private sector (see page 55). Some believe this is the ushering in of the "New Space Race." This means that Emily will continue to peel back the layers of wonder and marvel, explaining the findings that continue to develop and why they matter—and how they might affect not just us but future generations.

# PLANETARY ROVER

## TANYA HARRISON ROAMS MARS

# STANDING ON MARS

Here on Earth, Tanya Harrison often imagines she is on a Mars of the past. She can almost hear the trickle of its flowing rivers and see the lakes stretching out as far as she can see.

Did life once flourish on the now-barren planet? How can we use what we've learned about Mars—it was once wet and with a much thicker atmosphere than what exists today—and what we know about Earth to one day make the Red Planet our home?

For most of her career, these questions have propelled Tanya's passion to pull back the curtain on the mysteries of Mars, a planet that has sparked human curiosity for centuries.

# TANYA'S TIMELINE

**2006**

Graduates from the University of Washington with a Bachelor of Science in physics and astronomy

**1985**

Born in Seattle, Washington, USA

**2008**

Receives her master's degree from Wesleyan University in earth and environmental sciences

## 2016

Receives her PhD from Western University in geology with a specialization in planetary science and exploration

## 2017

Uses imaging to help determine the best landing site on Mars for the Perseverance rover

## 2018

Launches the first Women in Planetary Science and Exploration conference in Toronto (now called Women in Space)

# YOU NEED TO KNOW

## MARS ROVERS

Opportunity, Spirit, Curiosity, and Perseverance have conducted science experiments like analyzing materials from the surface of the planet.

## HISTORY OF MARS EXPLORATION

There have been more than 40 missions to the Red Planet by six countries—the United States, Russia (including the former Soviet Union), India, Japan, the United Arab Emirates, and China—as well as missions led by the European Space Agency.

## MARS RECONNAISSANCE ORBITER (MRO)

NASA spacecraft that reached Mars in 2006 and is used to monitor weather and climate and to find potential landing sites on the planet. It holds the most powerful camera ever flown to another planet.

# A HOME AWAY FROM HOME

From the moment Mars was recognized as a "wanderer" in ancient times—from which we get the Greek word for "planet"—humans have looked in awe at that red, starlike object traversing the sky, wandering among the stars.

The first attempts to orbit Mars were made by the former Soviet Union, now Russia, beginning in 1960. It would take until 1971 for the first spacecraft to successfully land on Mars—the Soviet Union's Mars 3. Of all the missions sent to Mars, a planet we know better than any other (aside from Earth, of course), fewer than half have been successful.

So why the continued drive to send spacecraft there? There's hope that someday humans will be able to call Mars home. Because of its relative proximity to Earth and its composition—it's rocky like Earth and has similar elements—it's the most promising planet we have to explore.

## MARTIAN "CANALS"

In 1609, famed Italian astronomer and inventor Galileo Galilei observed Mars using a telescope. In 1877, Giovanni Schiaparelli drew features he saw on Mars and labeled the channels *canali*. This was later misinterpreted to mean canals, which in turn led American astronomer Percival Lowell to believe they were carved out by an alien civilization.

The notion of living on Mars has taken a firm hold. The planet has numerous landers and rovers on its surface, and five countries—Russia, the United States, India, China, and the United Arab Emirates—have all sent satellites. NASA has plans to send humans to its surface, as does SpaceX, the first commercial company to aim for Mars.

## COMMERCIAL SPACE COMPANIES

Private companies, such as SpaceX and Blue Origin, aim to launch spacecraft into orbit or to the International Space Station.

But creating a new home on the Red Planet will be no easy task. First, getting there will be hard—space radiation threatens the health of astronauts during their six- to nine-month voyage. And then, how do we actually live there? Humans would have to adapt to their new life, learning self-sustenance and how to avoid dust storms and **Marsquakes** (earthquakes, but on Mars). Basically, they would have to learn a new way of living. There would be no stepping outside to bask in the sunlight or take deep breaths of fresh air. That's why so many countries, like the United States, are trying to learn more, and it's what Tanya has dedicated most of her career to: better understanding Mars.

## SPACE AND OUR BODIES

Space isn't made for humans. On Earth, we have the oxygen we need, our bodies receive the required sunlight and water, the temperatures are just right, and Earth's magnetic field protects us. Space, on the other hand, is a vacuum: exposed to it, we would die. Then there's radiation, including galactic cosmic radiation (GCR), which comes from the galaxy itself and is lethal to humans. To live in space—or even on a planet like Mars that doesn't have a magnetic field to shield us from radiation—we'd have to find ways to protect ourselves.

# WEATHER FORECASTS FOR MARS

On July 4, 1997, NASA's Mars Pathfinder spacecraft landed with the Sojourner rover on the dusty surface of Mars (see page 43). The images it sent back transfixed Tanya, who was just 11 years old. It was then that her love for the Red Planet was born. She studied physics and astronomy at university and then, hoping she could further study the rocky planet, went on to study geology. Her first Mars job was working for a company in California that collected images from NASA's Mars Reconnaissance Orbiter (MRO) in 2008.

You may not know it, but you've likely seen images from the MRO. The spacecraft orbits Mars with incredibly high-resolution cameras, providing unprecedented up-close images of the planet's terrain. All the hills, mountains, and valleys of the Red Planet—including the deepest valley and the tallest mountain in the solar system—are revealed in ways never seen before. But these images aren't just about pretty landscapes. They're about understanding the geology of Mars: what it was once like and what it's like now.

One of Tanya's roles there was choosing what one of the cameras would image over a week based on particularly interesting geological features. She then analyzed the images, studying the composition of the surface and looking for anything that stood out from its surroundings or seemed different.

But there was much more to her work: the weather of Mars. You might be surprised to know that the planet does have its own weather—and seasons—even though there may not be rain, thunderstorms, or hurricanes like here on Earth. The weather on Mars is mainly driven by wind, and because it's so dusty, it's important to understand how the wind can carry dust across the planet, particularly when there are rovers or landers on the surface that depend on sunlight to operate. If a solar panel is covered with dust, a rover's battery will die, and its mission will come to an end.

At the time, there were twin rovers—called Spirit and Opportunity—on the surface of Mars (see page 43). They had landed in 2004, and their mission was expected to last only about three months. But the two had already far outlived that timeline. Part of Tanya's job was using the MRO to monitor the Martian weather to ensure that the rovers would be safe. She also wrote daily weather reports and posted them online for the public.

Learning to understand the weather on Mars can help shape the path to choosing a suitable location for humans to visit or perhaps even live. Being armed with information on where dust storms are more likely to occur means that scientists can choose a safer location for humans to settle.

## AN ACCIDENTAL DISCOVERY

During its mission, Spirit had a few mishaps with its wheels, but they led to a great discovery. In 2006, one of its wheels was dragging as it moved across the surface of Mars. Scientists were shocked to discover that the broken wheel revealed something bright and white beneath the dusty surface. It was opaline silica. The presence of this mineral supported the theory that the region Spirit was in may have had hydrothermal activity in its distant past, where heat and water could have supported life.

# BENEATH THE SURFACE OF MARS

One of the reasons that Mars was so appealing to Tanya was that it is so Earth-like. From towering mountains to a canyon that runs like a deep scar across its landscape, to boulders and rocks and hills . . . Mars is Earth without the benefit of water. But Mars once *did* have water. And there's the belief that it still does. Some scientists believe that at one time most of the planet's northern hemisphere was a large ocean, and rivers flowed down hills and through valleys. And maybe, just maybe, it could have been suitable for life.

## EARTH VS. MARS

EARTH:

- circumference of roughly 40,030 kilometers (24,874 miles)
- weather that centers around water
- water ice at its poles
- thicker atmosphere than Mars
- stronger gravity than on Mars

MARS:

- circumference of 21,296 kilometers (13,233 miles)
- weather that centers around wind
- water ice at its poles
- thinner atmosphere than Earth
- weaker gravity than on Earth

What happened to that water? Where did it all go? Was there once life? Thanks in part to Tanya's research, we now know that the water may not have disappeared entirely.

One day at work in 2010, Tanya noticed what looked like a large outflow channel in one of the MRO images, similar to those that extend out from rivers here on Earth. There was no water there, of course, but it was very strange. She traced the channel back to a crater, and as she began to delve into more images, she realized something spectacular.

An entire network of channels seemed to originate from a particular crater in the northern plains of Mars. This wasn't an ancient crater that was made while our solar system was forming, with large rocks slamming into the Martian surface. No, this crater was far younger. In fact, it would have formed after the water on the surface of Mars had dried up billions of years ago.

This meant that whatever had slammed into Mars to make the crater had allowed groundwater to flow downward, forming the channel, or that the heat from the impact had melted large amounts of buried ice.

Water. There could be water beneath the surface of Mars. And if there was water at one point, there was a chance that it had created a warm, wet environment where life may have once thrived.

# BREAKING NEW GROUND

Like on Earth, Mars has different types of rocks that can tell us a lot about its past, which was very intriguing to Tanya. So, in 2012, she decided to leave her job and pursue a PhD in geology at Western University in London, Ontario, specializing in planetary science and exploration.

She didn't only want to learn about Mars; she also wanted to become a principal investigator, or PI, of a mission to Mars, a role that hadn't ever been held by a woman. This person is in charge of planning a space mission. They deal with the cost, science directives, and more. She believed that getting a PhD would help her in that goal.

However, when Tanya was very young, she was diagnosed with a life-altering condition called ankylosing spondylitis (AS), a type of arthritis that affects the spine and other joints. Sometimes this condition can cause bones to fuse together, causing a person extreme pain. While Tanya was at Western, her AS flared up, making it difficult to study. The pain was almost too much to bear; sometimes she would even be bedridden. But she refused to let the pain take over her life and continued to research and work from home.

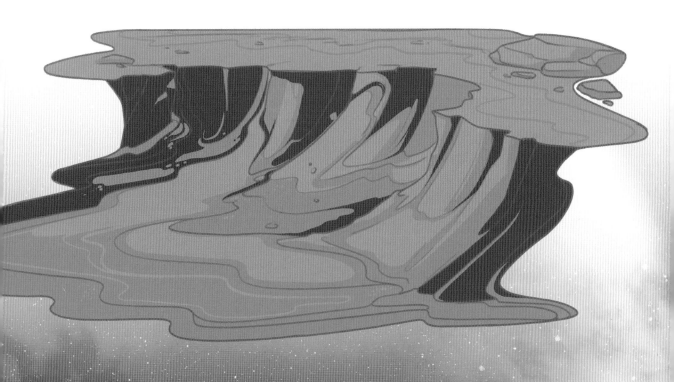

As part of her work, Tanya developed a very specific interest. During her years poring over roughly 75,000 MRO images of Mars, Tanya had become interested in gullies, landslides that can be triggered by a small amount of water, as they are here on Earth. She mapped out the location of every gully on Mars and looked for changes to see where new landslides had occurred. Out of about 5,000 different locations, she found 8 places where landslides had happened just over the past few years. This proved that Mars wasn't inactive; in fact, it was still very dynamic, with things changing often on the surface.

## ROBOT INVADERS!

Mars is the only planet in the solar system entirely populated by robots. The landers and rovers on Mars have become far more advanced over time. Sojourner, for example, was just 66 centimeters (26 inches) long, whereas Perseverance is 3 meters (roughly 10 feet) long, with far more instruments to study the planet in different ways. The rovers don't drive themselves but rather are programmed with a specific set of instructions from NASA that are relayed to Mars. These machines undergo rigorous tests on Earth under Mars-like conditions to ensure they will be able to operate when they arrive.

Tanya completed her PhD in record time and went on to a position at Arizona State University (ASU)—where she would once again work on Mars. She worked with the Opportunity rover in 2016, which was now the only twin still in operation. Spirit had gotten stuck and most of its wheels had jammed. It worked for a short time in place as a weather station for studying the interior of the planet before its mission officially ended in 2011. Tanya helped Oppy, who was getting on in age, analyze the scientific images that were requested.

NASA continued to send their hardworking rovers on missions to Mars, with Curiosity next in line. Tanya was part of a team of people who suggested landing sites for it. This rover, too, helped confirm the likelihood that Mars was once a habitable world by finding elements like sulfur, nitrogen, hydrogen, oxygen, phosphorus, and carbon, some of the key ingredients for life as we know it. Tanya worked on the color cameras for Curiosity (not all cameras on spacecraft are in color), the ones that send jaw-dropping images back home to Earth.

When preparing for the Perseverance mission, Tanya once again worked as a collaborator on the science team, helping source some of the best potential landing sites for the rover, ones that would be able to reveal more of Mars's history for planetary scientists, clues that might be trapped in the soil and rocks. The chosen location—Jezero Crater—was her top prospect, and Perseverance launched in July 2020.

The crater is significant to geologists like Tanya because billions of years ago, a river flowed into it, and it's possible that traces of past organic life—if there ever was life—could be trapped within that rock.

What's especially important about this landing location is that the rover will explore the Jezero Crater and collect samples of the soil. It will then package the samples and drop them on the surface of the planet. The plan is for a future rover to collect them and return them to Earth for scientists to analyze, something that's never been done before.

While it may not be as ideal as sending scientists to directly study the Martian surface, a sample-return mission is the next best thing. Thanks in part to Tanya's involvement—her past work with other rovers like Spirit, Opportunity, and Curiosity and her role in helping to choose candidate sites for Perseverance—those samples could potentially reveal things we've never known about the planet that has captured our attention for centuries. That information could shed light on what once was and what could be.

> " EACH MISSION WE SENT THERE UNLOCKED MORE PIECES TO THE PUZZLE OF THE PAST OF MARS, AND I WANT TO SEE HOW THE PUZZLE PANS OUT. "

# FROM MARS TO EARTH

In 2017, Tanya became an ambassador for Planet Labs, an Earth-imaging company that uses extremely high-resolution cameras on more than 200 satellites in orbit around Earth. The cameras are able to take photographs from space that measure just a few meters across. The company's goal is to monitor Earth on a daily basis, looking for any changes that occur over time. Their data helps with monitoring the climate, growing crops, and even disaster management. But their information can also be used to help us better understand Mars by looking at the geology of Earth.

From 2017 to 2018, Tanya used some of the Planet Labs data in her research at Arizona State University, using the Canadian Artic as an analogue for Mars. Some of the channels carved out by ice in the Arctic are very similar to those found on the now dry and dusty Red Planet. Tanya compared the two to see how the data from Earth could be used to further study Mars.

The following year, Tanya left ASU to join Planet Labs for good, where she now holds the title of Director of Strategic Science Initiatives. She views images of the only home we know, monitoring the effects of climate change, natural disasters, and even human rights abuses around the world, such as the bombing of villages.

She also formed her own company, Professional Martian LLC, which does science and science-fiction consulting. It's important to Tanya that movies and television shows get the science right. She aims to bring science to a wider audience and to make sure everyone is included in experiencing the wonder and awe she treasures every day.

On top of her day-to-day work, Tanya ensures that the voices of women in science are heard. She travels around the world giving talks and, together with fellow planetary scientists Sara Mazrouei and David Hamilton, created the Women in Space conference that unites women in the space industry. The first one took place in her favorite city, Toronto, in 2018. She is a top science communicator and is highly regarded around the world.

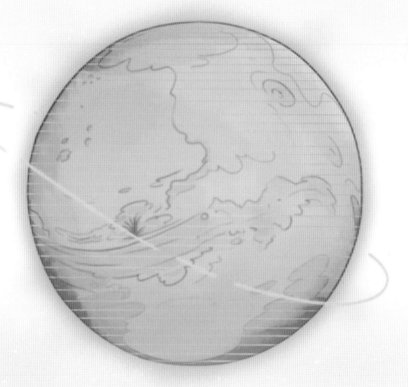

But Tanya hasn't ever truly left Mars. She has a wide following on social media, where she's known as @tanyaofmars. She shares her work, her findings, and her passion for a planet that humans have yet to set foot on, but it's one she has come to know intimately through her research.

Mars is the future, she says. And it's in the hands of your generation.

# LIFE BEYOND EARTH

## SARA SEAGER
## SEARCHES FOR ALIEN PLANETS

# DISTANT HORIZONS

Decades after Jill Tarter pioneered the use of radio signals to seek out cosmic company, we still haven't heard any signs of intelligent life. That doesn't necessarily mean that we're alone in the universe, though—we might just need a different way of searching. Enter the study of exoplanets: worlds orbiting a star other than our sun.

Of the eight planets in our solar system, Earth is the only planet confirmed to support life, even simple **microbial life** like bacteria or fungi. So if we want to find another habitable world, all we need to do is find another Earth—a different planet orbiting a different star, but one with similar conditions, chemistry, and composition. Just how challenging will that be? Our galaxy, the Milky Way, contains somewhere between 100 billion and 400 billion stars, and it is just one of over two trillion galaxies in the universe. The stars are tens to millions of **light-years** away from us, and our telescopes only do so much. And, more importantly, the planets are so faint compared to their bright, massive host stars. With such overwhelming numbers, it will take incredible minds and advanced new technology to even narrow down the possibilities, let alone actually find another Earth.

That's where Sara Seager comes in.

# SARA'S TIMELINE

**1971**
Born in Toronto, Ontario, Canada

**1994**
Graduates from the University of Toronto with a Bachelor of Science in mathematics and physics

**1999**
Receives her PhD in astronomy at Harvard University

**2007**
Becomes a professor at the Massachusetts Institute of Technology

## 2013

Is awarded a MacArthur Fellowship, often referred to as the "genius award"

## 2012

Is named one of *Time* magazine's 25 most influential people in space

## 2016

Becomes the Deputy Science Director of the Transiting Exoplanet Survey Satellite mission

# YOU NEED TO KNOW

### LIGHT-YEAR

The distance light travels in one Earth year. One light-year is roughly nine trillion kilometers (five and a half trillion miles).

### TESS

Launched in 2018, the Transiting Exoplanet Survey Satellite telescope searches for exoplanets, surveying roughly 200,000 of the brightest stars near Earth. It can scan an area 400 times larger than the Kepler space telescope.

### EXOPLANET

A planet outside our solar system that orbits a star other than our sun

### KEPLER SPACE TELESCOPE

A telescope that launched in 2009, whose sole purpose was to look for planets using a special camera that measured the brightness of stars and their potential dimming by a planet crossing in front of them.

# DISCOVERING EXOPLANETS

Sara was working on her PhD at Harvard at a time when scientists were making monumental discoveries—the first exoplanets. When it came time for Sara to write her **thesis**, her adviser suggested she research 51 Pegasi b—one of the newly discovered exoplanets. It was a daunting task, but Sara welcomed it. Her thesis focused on hot extrasolar giant planets, what are more commonly referred to as "hot Jupiters." These giant exoplanets orbit very close to their parent star.

Even though the existence of exoplanets was officially confirmed, many astronomers saw the study of them as somewhat fanciful—something out of science fiction. What were the odds of finding more of them? And what could we hope to learn from planets so far away we couldn't even see them? At conferences, students from other universities suggested to Sara that she should pursue a more "serious" area of study. Luckily, Sara wasn't dissuaded. She knew that by searching for exoplanets and studying their size, temperature, and atmosphere, she could help uncover the secrets of planetary formation and try to answer a critical question: Is Earth a fluke—or could there be another Earth-like planet out there?

## THE FIRST EXOPLANETS

In 1992, the astronomers Alex Wolszczan and Dale Frail announced a historic discovery: two exoplanets roughly 2,000 light-years away, orbiting a pulsar, a small, dense star that gives off strong pulses of radiation in regular patterns, like a lighthouse among the stars.

This discovery was monumental, but it didn't necessarily mean life could exist on distant worlds. Pulsars give off enormous amounts of harmful radiation that would likely prevent life from arising on any planet orbiting them.

Just a few years later, however—in 1995—an exoplanet called 51 Pegasi b was discovered orbiting a sunlike star, another first. The planet is roughly the same mass as Jupiter and is relatively close, just 50 light-years away.

With trillions of stars in the universe, each of them with possible planets in orbit, one of the biggest questions Sara faced was how to find what she was looking for. The first two exoplanets were discovered when astronomers noticed that the pulses of radiation given off by a star in regular intervals were being disrupted, indicating that something was physically blocking the radiation. On the other hand, 51 Pegasi b was discovered when astronomers identified a wobble in a star, showing that its orbit was disturbed by something.

## MICROBIAL LIFE

Consists of simple life-forms that include bacteria, viruses, algae, and fungi, among others

But in 1999, right after Sara finished her PhD, astronomers found a new way to study exoplanets when they confirmed the existence of planet HD 209458 b using the transit method. This method involves regularly measuring the brightness of a star with a telescope, looking for any temporary drops in brightness. The slightest dip, even just 1 percent, is a sign that an orbiting planet might be passing in front of the star, blocking its light. Sara showed that by also measuring the way that light moves through a planet's atmosphere, the transit method can tell astronomers about the atmosphere's chemical makeup and how similar it might be to Earth's—a crucial component in determining if a planet might host life. This new idea helped lead to the first detection of an atmosphere around an exoplanet. Sara also helped discover the first light emitted from an exoplanet.

For a planet to be potentially habitable, it must have liquid water at its surface. But most planets don't pass this test. To add an extra challenge, there's only so much astronomers can actually tell about exoplanets because they are so far away. That's why Sara works to characterize exoplanets using their atmospheres—which are the easiest to see and measure. Sara looks for atmospheric gases like water vapor, ozone, oxygen, and carbon dioxide.

In 2009, Sara's work received a huge boost with the launch of a revolutionary new tool: the Kepler space telescope, dedicated entirely to searching for exoplanets using the transit method. It continuously monitored more than 150,000 stars near Earth's location in the Milky Way and sent data back to Earth to be analyzed by astronomers looking for that characteristic dip in a star's brightness.

Astronomers used data from the Kepler telescope to discover all kinds of planets, including some types not found in our own solar system: sub-Neptune-sized planets, which are now believed to be the most common type of planet in our galaxy, as well as hot Jupiters like the ones Sara had studied during her PhD. By the time Kepler used up all its fuel in 2018, it had discovered more than 2,600 exoplanets, with plenty of data still left for Sara to keep analyzing.

It turns out our galaxy is brimming with distant worlds.

## PEERING AT ATMOSPHERES OF FAR-OFF WORLDS

To determine the composition of an exoplanet's atmosphere, scientists use a method called spectroscopy, which splits light up into different wavelengths. Different wavelengths of visible light correspond to different colors. As light from its star passes through a planet's atmosphere, the light's wavelengths can be absorbed by the different gas molecules present. Different gases absorb different wavelengths of light. Whatever wavelengths aren't absorbed can be seen as particular colors. When it comes to searching for Earth-like planets, scientists are looking for gases like carbon dioxide and water vapor along with biosignature gases—such ammonia, oxygen, and nitrous oxide—which are produced by life and build up in the atmosphere.

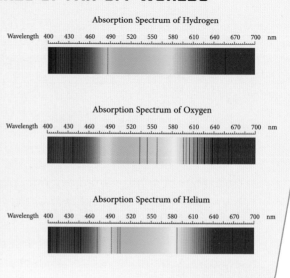

# HER OWN EQUATION

The hunt for exoplanets recently added a new player: NASA's Transiting Exoplanet Survey Satellite (TESS) mission, where Sara was the deputy science director until August 2020. Launched in 2018, the TESS space telescope is a monster exoplanet hunter. It's built to search over 85 percent of the sky, rather than focusing on just a portion as Kepler did, and it is set to study 200,000 of the brightest nearby stars. Because TESS observes stars closer to Earth than those monitored by Kepler, ground-based telescopes will be able to offer follow-up observations, potentially helping to confirm possible exoplanets.

Using data from Kepler and TESS, Sara has helped refine something called the **habitable zone**—the area surrounding a star where it would be possible for liquid water to exist on the surface of a planet.

## THE HABITABLE ZONE

In order for a planet to support life as we know it, it needs to have liquid water on its surface. The habitable zone is the relative region around a star where this is possible. If a planet is too close to its star, the water will boil off and evaporate. If the planet is too far away, the water will freeze. Of course, it also depends on the type of star—some stars burn hotter and brighter than others, which affects the relative distance and location of the habitable zone.

Using the idea of the Drake Equation, the formula for estimating how many alien civilizations capable of radio communication might exist in our galaxy (see page 28), Sara has created a formula of her own. The Seager Equation estimates the number of planets that could be detectable from Earth via biosignature gases—gases that are produced by life. It looks like this:

$N = N*F_Q F_{HZ} F_O F_L F_S$

where

$N$ = the number of planets with detectable signs of life via biosignature gases

$N*$ = the number of stars observed

$F_Q$ = the fraction of stars that are quiet

$F_{HZ}$ = the fraction of stars with rocky planets in the habitable zone

$F_O$ = the fraction of those planets that can be observed

$F_L$ = the fraction of planets that have life

$F_S$ = the fraction of planets on which life produces a detectable signature gas

The result? By using values based on a specific type of star most common in our corner of the galaxy the Seager Equation determines that two habitable planets could be discovered out of the planets found by the TESS mission.

# STARLIGHT, STARSHADE

So what's next?

We now know that alien worlds exist, and we can study the atmospheres of a wide variety of exoplanets. But small, rocky worlds like our own have atmospheres that are much more difficult to see because they are tiny against the backdrop of the host star. And exoplanets in general are incredibly difficult to photograph for the same reason.

But what if you could block that light just as a moon blocks out the sun during a solar eclipse? That's the concept Sara is working on with NASA—a starshade. The idea was first suggested by astronomer Lyman Spitzer in 1962. It sounds simple in theory: all you need is an object to hold up in front of the star to screen its light. But the reality is much more complicated.

A starshade mission would require two spacecraft working together—one would be the telescope searching for exoplanets, and the other would carry the starshade. In order for the shade to work, it would have to be tens of meters in diameter—not exactly an easy thing to get into space. It would also need to fly at a distance of 20,000 to 40,000 kilometers (12,427 to 24,855 miles) in front of the telescope. To put that in perspective, Michael Bottom, a NASA engineer, explained it like this: If the starshade was the size of a coaster, the telescope would be the size of a pencil eraser, and the pair would be separated by a distance of about 100 kilometers (62 miles). On top of that, they would need to be closely aligned.

The shade also has to be shaped in a way that works with the way that light moves. A circle won't work because light would still show around the edges. Instead, the starshade design looks like a giant sunflower. The shape of the petals would block the starlight from reaching the telescope but still allow astronomers to see the light coming from the exoplanet itself. This would let astronomers take pictures of it and study its atmosphere, providing Sara with more clues as to the planet's composition.

## COOLEST EXOPLANETS EVER FOUND

No two planets in our solar system are the same. There's the ringed Saturn, dusty Mars, gigantic Jupiter, and Uranus, rotating on its side. But out among the different stars are wild and wonderful planets we could never have dreamed of. There's a planet as dark as coal, planets orbiting two stars, and even one orbiting around a star that is eating it.

# BRAVE NEW WORLDS

Kepler and TESS will not be the last space telescopes that search for exoplanets. There are plans for bigger and more advanced telescopes to find these worlds. The James Webb Space Telescope will study exoplanets and their atmospheres at a specific set of **wavelengths**—the infrared, which is undetectable to the human eye—giving it the ability to see exoplanets in a different class: Saturn-like planets that are smaller than Jupiter and are father away from their host star. Something that astronomers are particularly keen on is the telescope's ability to study the properties—both physical and chemical—of potential exoplanets, something that at the moment is nearly impossible to do. It may even take photographs of these distant worlds.

> " PART OF THE JOY OF SCIENCE IS DISCOVERY. "

The Nancy Grace Roman Space Telescope—named after the first chief astronomer at NASA for her role in the development of the **Hubble Space Telescope**—will use new technology, such as a camera with a wider field of view than other telescopes use. It will also be able to better look for planets around distant stars and to discover roughly 2,600 new exoplanets.

In a crucial development in the study of potentially habitable worlds, Sara was recently part of an incredible discovery that brought her search much closer to home.

When looking at atmospheres in the search for potentially habitable planets, a particular chemical compound—phosphine—is considered a good indicator, as it is a strong biosignature gas. In 2020, Jane Greaves, an astronomer based in the United Kingdom, published a paper about phosphine in the clouds of Venus. This gas is associated with life here on Earth, and astronomers theorize that it could be associated with life on other planets.

Sara's team was already working on the possibility that phosphine could be detected in the atmospheres of exoplanets. Her team joined Jane Greaves's team and showed that no natural phenomenon, such as volcanoes or lightning, could produce such an amount, and no known chemistry could explain it. The only thing left was the potential existence of life in the clouds of Venus. Much like the early speculation about the existence of exoplanets, life on Venus sounds like science fiction. To have it suddenly emerge as a serious possibility shook the entire astronomical community.

In August 2020, Sara and six other scientists revisited the possibility of life on Venus and published a paper together. In it, they suggested that microbial life might be contained within liquid droplets found in the clouds surrounding the planet.

However, further research by several independent astronomers suggests that the amount of gas detected may not be as high as initially reported. Still, the team of researchers say it is an exciting discovery that calls for a mission to analyze the atmosphere of Venus.

When Sara first began studying to become an astronomer 30 years ago, exoplanets were just a theory—one that didn't receive much support from the scientific community. By 2022, more than 5,000 exoplanets had been confirmed, with more than 5,400 awaiting confirmation and more than 3,100 planetary systems identified out in the stars. Today, it's estimated that each star in the universe is home to, on average, three planets. We've gone from knowing next to nothing to being ever closer to finding another Earth—and the possibilities keep expanding.

The next generation of astronomers will have the chance to follow in Sara's footsteps; they will likely be the ones to find life far beyond our solar system, using technology that we have yet to even imagine.

Who knows? You could be the one to make the discovery.

## SEXISM IN STEM

Sara was in attendance at the 2017 Starmus Festival, an international astronomy, science, and arts festival, when the Nobel Prize–winning economist Sir Christopher Pissarides claimed that Apple's digital assistant, Siri, is more trustworthy when it uses a man's voice instead of a woman's. It was a shock and an insult. Jill Tarter, who was also in attendance, stood up and walked out, along with Sara and many other women. Regrettably, this is just the tip of the iceberg. In some cases, sexism, racism, and other barriers prevent women and non-binary people from pursuing science in the first place. Until we break down these barriers, we'll never know what kinds of discoveries we might be missing out on.

# RUNNING HOT OR COLD

## RENÉE HLOŽEK PREDICTS HOW THE UNIVERSE WILL END

# THE BIG PICTURE

So far, we've talked about exoplanets, the possibility of intelligent life, and our first attempts at space exploration. But what about the BIG picture? How did it all start? How did the stars, galaxies, and planets get here in the first place? How did we? And how long will everything last?

Renée Hložek is working to answer some of the most complicated questions we can ask about our existence—and the existence of the universe itself. Looking out from our planet, her gaze extends beyond the reaches of our solar system and even our galaxy. Renée studies the billions of galaxies that make up our universe to try to predict the future: what may happen soon, what may follow after that, and ultimately, how our universe might come to an end. After all, nothing lasts forever.

# RENÉE'S TIMELINE

**2013**

Becomes a TED Senior Fellow, bringing astrophysics concepts to a global audience

**2011**

Earns her PhD at the University of Oxford as a Rhodes Scholar

**1983**

Born in Pretoria, South Africa

## 2013

Creates the Hope-Princeton exchange to help bring South African women scientists, including astrophysicists, to study at Princeton

## 2020

As part of an international team, uses the Atacama Cosmology Telescope to support the age of the universe as being roughly 13.8 billion years old

# YOU NEED TO KNOW

### THE BIG BANG

The moment the universe began

### COSMOLOGY

The study of the universe

### DARK ENERGY

The force that is causing the universe to expand faster and faster

### DARK MATTER

An invisible part of the universe whose presence is known only by how it interacts gravitationally with other objects

### GRAVITY

The force by which a planet or celestial body—such as a star or moon—pulls objects toward its center

# IN THE BEGINNING . . .

Roughly 13.8 billion years ago, all of the matter that exists today was once much closer together, a hot, dense plasma made of tiny particles mixed with light and energy—it was called a singularity. It is easy to think that the **Big Bang** exploded out from one point in space, but space itself was smaller, so the Big Bang happened everywhere in the universe at the same time.

That single point expanded at the **speed of light**, giving birth to the earliest version of the universe.

## THE SPEED OF LIGHT

The speed of light is measured in terms of how long it takes light to travel through a vacuum, which is 299,792,458 meters (983,571,056 feet) per second—or 300,000 kilometers (186,000 miles) per second.

The tiny particles came together to form **atoms**, the building blocks of the universe. Those atoms grouped together to eventually form **molecules**. Stars and galaxies were created, and as the universe expanded, it cooled and became luminous. This is the beginning of the universe according to the Big Bang theory.

Everything that makes the universe what it is—and everything that makes you you—started with the Big Bang. But even if we have a theory as to the universe's scientific origin story, there are still so many mysteries to unlock. How do we explain the things we can't see?

## GALAXIES AND OUR UNIVERSE

Galaxies are collections of billions of stars, planets, gas, and dust, all held together by gravity. The universe is everything that exists, including galaxies, stars, planets, energy, and time. It is estimated that there are roughly 200 billion galaxies in our universe.

For example, we know that Earth orbits the sun at a mind-blowing 110,000 kilometers per hour (67,000 miles per hour), and the sun orbits the center of our galaxy at 828,000 kilometers per hour (515,000 miles per hour). Even galaxies can orbit one another. At those high speeds, stars and planets should fling out from their parent galaxies if they were held in orbit only by the gravity of their visible masses. Instead, since planets, stars, and galaxies all remain in orbit, there must be something keeping the contents of the universe together—even if we can't see exactly what it is.

In 1933, the Swiss astronomer Fritz Zwicky coined the term **dark matter** to refer to the invisible mass in the universe that acts as a sort of cosmic glue. It can only be seen through the way it interacts with other objects. One example of this is called gravitational lensing, where the dense gravity of dark matter bends light that passes nearby.

## THE DISCOVERY OF DARK MATTER

**1933:** Fritz Zwicky discovers that a cluster of galaxies only has about 1 percent of the mass needed to keep the galaxies from escaping the cluster's gravity. He theorizes that there must be "missing mass" in the universe.

**1948:** Ralph Alpher theorizes that there should be leftover radiation from the creation of the universe.

**1964:** Arno Penzias and Robert Wilson discover the cosmic microwave background (CMB).

**1974:** Similar to Zwicky's discovery, the astronomers Vera Rubin and W. Kent Ford find within galaxies that visible stars make up just 10 percent of the mass needed to keep stars from flying out, escaping the pull of their host galaxy. While planets orbit more slowly the farther they are from their star, the astronomers discover that the stars at the farthest reach of a galaxy don't slow down as they orbit the center of their galaxies.

Astronomers have also determined that dark matter makes up about 27 percent of the universe. Most of the remaining universe—about 68 percent—is **dark energy**. Unlike dark matter, it doesn't pull things together. Instead, it pushes the universe apart and causes it to expand. This means that even though it may seem like there are infinite stars in the night sky, all of the visible elements of the universe—from stars to planets and comets to asteroids—only make up 5 percent of what's out there. Although astronomers believe they are close to an answer, 90 years after Zwicky's initial discovery, we still don't know exactly what makes up dark matter or dark energy.

So why does it matter what the universe is made of? Remember the Big Bang?

When all those stars and galaxies formed—billions of them—they started moving away from one another. We call that expansion. Because of the way dark energy behaves, the more the universe expands, the more that dark energy also expands. However, the visible parts of our universe and dark matter do not expand in the same way. What will happen as dark energy continues to grow and the universe continues to expand? By uncovering more about what makes up our universe and how dark matter and dark energy work, we learn not only about the universe's origin point but also about where we're heading—and how the universe will eventually end. For Renée and her fellow **cosmologists**, this is the ultimate puzzle.

### THE EXPANSION OF OUR UNIVERSE

The universe has continued to expand since the Big Bang. It's believed that something is making it expand faster than astronomers once thought—dark energy. An easy way to illustrate the expansion is to imagine a balloon with dots marked all over it. The more air you breathe into the balloon, the farther away the dots move away from one another.

# SO, HOW *WILL* IT END?

Fortunately, Renée has always loved puzzles. Even as a child, she preferred problem-solving over simple games, using perseverance and something halfway between patience and stubbornness to work her way toward answers. Those same traits fueled Renée's studies in mathematics and science and have driven her work in trying to unravel the mysteries of dark matter, dark energy, and the possible paths to the universe's end.

While it's true that we have more urgent scientific concerns—like slowing the effects of climate change, for example—it's also true that the future of the universe is our future as well. The more we know about the universe, the more we understand about our own past, and the more clearly we can imagine the future. And as we learn, we develop new theories, new technologies, and new ways of figuring out the truth.

But here's the thing about studying the question of how the universe will end: there's no clear-cut answer. Here are a few theories, with some pretty cool names:

1.  The Big Crunch: The universe will stop expanding and will collapse upon itself.

2.  The Big Rip: Everything in the universe will be torn apart due to its rapid expansion.

3.  Vacuum Decay: The Higgs Field, which surrounds our universe and gives things their mass, will become unstable. This will create a bubble of universe with completely new laws of physics. As this bubble expands at the speed of light throughout the universe, it will destroy everything it encounters.

4.  Heat Death: Dark energy will cause the universe to expand forever. As it expands, it will become colder and colder, eventually running out of gas to form stars or anything at all.

These are some pretty apocalyptic-sounding possibilities, but fear not: these and other theories predict that the end won't come for billions upon billions upon billions of years.

Renée focuses particularly on the heat death theory. But as you can imagine, it's hard to solve a mystery when you can't actually see the clues. This incredible detective work is at the heart of Renée's job.

# BACK TO THE BEGINNING

After completing her PhD, one of Renée's first jobs involved analyzing images taken by a telescope to study the cosmic microwave background radiation—one of the key ways cosmologists can see backward in time.

Whenever you look at anything up in the sky, you are looking at things not as they are but as they were. The light from the sun (don't ever look directly at it!) is 8 minutes old due to the time it takes light to travel (remember the speed of light?). Light from the moon takes 1.25 seconds to reach us. The farther out you go, the longer it takes. Light from Alpha Centauri, the closest star system to Earth, takes 4.3 years. Light from the closest spiral galaxy to Earth takes 2.5 million years, and so on.

The farthest astronomers have ever been able to see is 13.2 billion light-years away, shortly after the universe was born, meaning the light took that long to reach us. But we can get even closer to seeing the beginning of the universe by studying the cosmic microwave background (CMB) radiation. The CMB is a by-product of the Big Bang. The rapid period of inflation that marked the beginning of the universe generated a lot of heat, and that heat is represented by the CMB.

In 1989, NASA launched the Cosmic Background Explorer in order to map the CMB. The first image was released in 1992. Like looking at sunlight piercing through the clouds, the image showed leftover radiation 400,000 years after the Big Bang, showing mostly a uniform radiation, or temperature, with some hot spots. While this may sound like a long time ago, you need to remember just how old the universe is. Looking at an image 400,000 years after the Big Bang is like looking at a baby photo of the universe—our origin point.

## ADVANCEMENTS IN IMAGING CMB

In 1948, astronomer Ralph Alpher predicted that there must be radiation remaining from the Big Bang. In 1964, two scientists, Arno Penzias and Robert Wilson, who worked for Bell Telephone Laboratories, tried to set up a radio telescope. The incredibly sensitive telescope kept picking up an unknown signal, day and night. They cleaned the antenna, thinking it might be pigeon droppings, but the signal never stopped. Eventually, they realized that it was cosmic microwave radiation. NASA began mapping the CMB in 1989 with the launch of the Cosmic Background Explorer and released the first image of the CMB in 1992.

As camera technology has improved over time, so has the quality of the images of the CMB we've been able to capture. The Wilkinson Microwave Anisotropy Probe, launched in 2001, represented the first big jump in image quality and precision, followed by the Planck space telescope, launched by the European Space Agency in 2009.

> " WE LIVE AT AN EXTRAORDINARY TIME IN THE LIFE OF THE UNIVERSE WHERE WE CAN START TO UNDERSTAND THE UNIVERSE'S JOURNEY. "

# COSMIC CANDLES LIGHT THE WAY

Okay, now we know that we can look back in time, but how exactly does that help Renée? She uses data and images from the Atacama Cosmology Telescope (ACT) in Chile in her research. The ACT observes cosmic microwave radiation at such a high resolution that even distant, ancient galaxy clusters can be detected. This allows Renée to see the universe at its earliest state.

Renée then uses different methods to calculate the expansion of the universe. One method involves studying a particular kind of stellar explosion called a type Ia supernova. These explosions happen when a **white dwarf star** and another star orbit around each other. Over time, the white dwarf star pulls material off the other star until it becomes so dense that it can't resist the crush of its own gravity. The resulting explosion of the white dwarf star is often brighter than its parent galaxy, making it easy to see by telescope even from very far away.

## WHITE DWARF STARS

A small, dense star that is created when a larger star runs out of fuel. When this happens, the star expels its outer layers so only its core remains. Our sun will eventually become a white dwarf star.

Because white dwarf stars tend to be composed of similar chemicals and have similar mass, the brightness and mass they produce when they explode also tend to be similar from one star to the next. These Ia supernovae are known as cosmic standard candles—markers that help Renée calculate distance in space. Because she can measure both how bright such a supernova actually is and how bright it appears to us here on Earth, Renée can tell how far away it is—and the farther away a supernova is, the further back into the past the star actually exploded.

In this way, the tiniest details—like the relative brightness of individual stars exploding—help Renée answer the biggest questions. By looking at images of cosmic standard candles at different distances, and images that map the CMB, she is looking at the universe across many different stages of its past. By charting the ways the universe has changed over time, Renée gets ever closer to learning the secrets of dark matter and dark energy and to unlocking the as-yet-unknowable 95 percent of our universe.

Her efforts will soon get an extra boost from a new telescope coming onto the scene. While the ACT that Renée currently relies on maps around 200 square degrees of the sky, the Legacy Survey of Space and Time (LSST)—located at the Vera C. Rubin Observatory in Chile—will survey the entire sky every few days over a period of 10 years. This will give Renée and her fellow cosmologists an unprecedented amount of data to work with. Renée is also involved with this project through developing new techniques to use the data in the best way possible to understand dark energy.

# THE WORK OF LIFETIMES

Why even bother trying to determine how the universe will end? After all, it's highly unlikely that it will happen anytime soon, so why should we care?

You can think of Renée's work—observing what the universe looked like in the past—in the same way you would look at photos or videos of yourself from when you were younger: you may see hints about who you were growing up to become—your interests, your likes and dislikes, and your personality traits. The more photos you have,

the more hints you might spot. In the same way, the more data and images we have to help us understand how the universe has grown and changed so far, the better the chances for scientists like Renée to predict what our universe might be like in the future.

Renée's work is the work of lifetimes. While we may soon know more about what dark matter and dark energy are, it will likely take us hundreds if not thousands of years to unlock the secrets of the universe—and there's no guarantee that we'll get there. By laying out the groundwork now, Renée is building a foundation for the generation of scientists that will come after her. Maybe you will join them and do the same for the generation that follows you. In this way, the natural spark of human curiosity becomes a torch that gradually illuminates the cosmic mysteries that surround us. We can only guess at everything we still have to learn.

# PEERING THROUGH THE CLOUDS

## ASHLEY WALKER
### AND THE MAKING OF OTHER WORLDS

# COMING OUT OF THE CLOUDS

More than five billion years ago, where you're sitting right now was nothing but a swirling cloud of rocks, dust, and gas. There was no Earth. In fact, there were no planets at all. No moons either. Just a newly born star, shining brightly, with rocks and dust circling it. Over time, those rocks and dust and gas would begin to crash into one another, some sticking together, some not, eventually forming new worlds that are the planets and moons we know today.

Each world that emerged is unique. There are the rocky worlds, the inner planets—Earth with its mountains, oceans, and abundance of life; Mercury with its cratered surface; Venus with its thick atmosphere; and Mars, a world that once may have had an ocean but is now dust and rocks. Then there are the outer planets—Saturn with its breathtaking rings; Jupiter with its turbulent clouds and storms; and the large, icy gas giants, Uranus and Neptune. And there are hundreds of moons, both large and small.

And while it may seem that these worlds are far too distant from any of the light and warmth of the sun that we need to survive, the fact is that we've only recently discovered organisms that can survive in the harshest regions of Earth with little sunlight or even little oxygen, things that we believe are needed for life. These types of organisms are called **extremophiles**.

# ASHLEY'S TIMELINE

**2018-2019**

Interns and is a visiting student at John Hopkins University studying the prebiotic chemistry of Titan, one of Saturn's moons

**2017**

Interns at the Harvard & Smithsonian Center for Astrophysics studying ice chemistry in planet-forming regions

**1988**

Born in Evergreen Park, Illinois, USA

## 2020
Interns at NASA's Goddard Space Flight Center studying Titan's ice cloud chemistry

## 2021
Begins position as a Graduate Research Assistant at Howard University

## 2022
Begins doctoral studies at Howard University

## 2020
Founds #BlackInAstro and co-founds #BlackInChem and #BlackInPhysics to raise awareness about the work done by Black scientists in their respective fields

# YOU NEED TO KNOW

## ASTROCHEMISTRY

The study of the structures, compositions, properties, and reactions of the different elements that make up space

## PREBIOTIC ASTROCHEMISTRY

The study of molecules and chemical reactions that lead to life on planets or moons

## TITAN

Saturn has more than 82 known moons, but one of the most spectacular is Titan. It is the largest of the Saturnian system and the only other world in our solar system that has weather patterns similar to Earth's.

Of all of these worlds, only one would see life thrive: Earth. But over time, especially within the past few decades, we have come to learn that not all is as it seems. Mars could have once had life, and perhaps it might still. There's some belief that Venus might have life in its clouds (see page 74). And Titan, Saturn's mightiest moon, is a moon like no other: it has an atmosphere and a weather system similar to our own.

Today, scientists are hopeful that we will send spacecraft to further explore Venus and Titan because there is so much they can tell us, even about our own planet's early formation. And that is why Ashley Walker has her head stuck in the clouds.

## THE CASSINI MISSION

In 1997, the Cassini spacecraft launched into space. Its destination: Saturn. Cassini would forever change our view of Saturn and its moons. After it arrived in 2004, it spent 13 years exploring the planetary system, documenting massive storms, exploring its intricate ring system, and even discovering other small moons, or moonlets. But Cassini also had a passenger, Huygens, a spacecraft built by the European Space Agency. In 2005, Huygens descended through the clouds of Saturn's largest moon, Titan, and revealed a world like no other we'd ever seen—one with lakes and rivers and weathered rocks, the kind you might find near a stream. The joint Cassini-Huygens mission will go down in history as one of the most successful space missions ever.

# DANCING TO THE STARS

Ashley didn't always have her head in the clouds, but she did love our universe from an early age. She once asked her mother to buy her a star, and she even said that she wanted to be the moon. Not *go* to the moon but actually *be* the moon.

Her love continued after her uncle got Ashley her first telescope, but it eventually waned while she was in high school. Instead, she became more focused on dance, hoping to one day become a choreographer, and she dreamed of opening her own dance studio.

She decided to study business, but one day she was watching the television show *Criminal Minds*, a series that focused on profiling suspects of various crimes. She became interested in forensics, where scientists use laboratory analysis to solve a crime. It inspired her to make a switch to studying chemistry.

The universe was still in her heart, and she longed to uncover some of its mysteries. So with the encouragement of a mentor, she decided to study astronomy as a major together with chemistry.

Instead of dancing on stage, Ashley was dancing among the stars.

# HOW DO YOU BUILD A HABITABLE PLANET?

We've talked a lot about all the research currently being done on exoplanets (see page 68), distant worlds orbiting distant stars. It's a relatively new branch of astronomy that has seen a lot of development in recent years, mainly due to the advance of technology that makes detecting these worlds somewhat easier. Scientists have learned a lot about the makeup and environments of the foreign planets we've encountered. Some are largely made of diamond, while others rain glass. Some are big and puffy—others, small and rocky.

But of all the elements that can make up a planet, what are the ones that allow life to thrive? What are the chemical combinations that make a planet potentially habitable? How does life arise and under what conditions? Ashley is intrigued by all the possibilities these questions present. She's an astrochemist, a scientist who studies the chemistry of cosmological bodies and space. In particular, she's studying the giant moon Titan and its thick, cloudy atmosphere because, though no life has been detected as of yet, some astronomers believe this moon could be a great place to find it.

### TITAN

Titan is the solar system's second-largest moon, following Jupiter's moon Ganymede. Of the more than 200 moons in our solar system, Titan is the only one we know of that has a thick atmosphere. It also has weather patterns, including rain and storms—though its rain is more like gasoline. Titan is also icy, like so many moons of the outer solar system. Beneath the ice, astronomers believe, could be a liquid ocean that may hold life, but we don't yet know its chemistry. Of course, it may be lifeless, but either way, the moon is so unique that astronomers are eager to explore it.

Titan—a moon slightly larger than our own—has long fascinated astronomers. When the Voyager spacecraft flew by it in the early 1980s, it showed a world covered in clouds that hid its surface. Since then, we've learned that the moon's atmosphere is composed mostly of nitrogen (like Earth's) but with clouds, rivers, lakes, and seas of chemicals like methane and ethane, which are similar to gasoline. And it's believed that it might also have a **subsurface ocean**.

Ashley studies the chemistry of Titan's clouds in a laboratory. She creates tholins, organic compounds found in Titan's atmosphere that consist mostly of carbon, nitrogen, and methane, and irradiates them with ultraviolet rays in a special box. Then she analyzes what molecules are created. The simulation is so accurate that the haze in the laboratory looks just like the haze in Titan's atmosphere, a deep orange.

The molecules that Ashley creates in her lab can tell her more about what might exist on the surface of the giant moon, and what could exist on exoplanets or even make them potentially habitable.

Because water is essential for life on Earth, it's driven our exploration of other planets and moons. Scientists have a saying: "Follow the water." It means that in the search for life or habitable worlds, we look for planets and moons with water. In particular,

## SUBSURFACE OCEAN

An ocean that lies beneath the crust of a planet or moon. In addition to Titan, astronomers believe that Enceladus, a moon around Saturn, and Europa, a moon around Jupiter, both have subsurface oceans.

scientists look for water to exist on the surface. But any life that exists or arises beyond Earth may be chemically different from what we know of here. And that's part of what makes this research so interesting for Ashley.

"I want to understand more about . . . planetary habitability because each planet, each planetary atmosphere and habitability, is different, unique from the next," she says.

Ashley also uses computer simulations to ascertain what these chemical compositions could lead to. It's like making substitutions in a recipe: different ingredients lead to different results. And yes, she's even wondering if life could exist on the surface of Titan. Because there the "water" exists in the form of methane lakes, it wouldn't support any life we've ever seen. It would be life that could only exist in the most extreme conditions. There could even be life that exists in the potential subsurface ocean.

But what's most exciting for Ashley is a mission to Titan scheduled for 2027 that will have a robotic rotorcraft—similar to a helicopter—called Dragonfly that will fly around the icy moon. It will be the first dedicated mission of a flying craft on another world. It will look for the building blocks of life, prebiotic chemical processes, and other clues as to whether or not life could have once existed or could still exist.

Ashley imagines Dragonfly soaring above the dunes, rivers, and weathered rocks of Titan, doing the research she can't physically do herself on the shrouded moon. She knows she'll have to be patient, but she can't wait to find out what secrets Titan is hiding.

## DRAGONFLY

First, humans sent spacecraft to fly by other planets. Then we designed spacecraft that could orbit them. Eventually, we sent landers and rovers, machines that can move across the face of a planet, like on Mars. Now, scientists have upped their game: they're sending machines that can fly around a planet, just as helicopters and planes do. The first of its kind was Ingenuity, a helicopter that piggybacked a ride on the Mars Perseverance mission. The numerous flights were highly successful. Now, engineers are preparing to send Dragonfly, a rotorcraft that will look at dozens of locations NASA believes might shed some light on whether or not life exists. The spacecraft is scheduled to launch in 2027 and arrive in 2035. Scientists also hope that it will provide clues as to how life arose on Earth.

# SEEING THE FUTURE IN THE PAST

While Ashley is uncovering the complex chemistry on Titan and its potential habitability, she's also intrigued by the very first clouds—the swirling clouds of debris that first created our solar system, its planets, and eventually us.

Those clouds—called protoplanetary disks—are believed to be what creates all planetary systems. Ashley wants to understand not only our own early protoplanetary disk and what that may have looked like but also how other protoplanetary disks might look. She wants to know what the protoplanetary disks of other known planetary systems might have looked like in their distant past. By looking at them, she would be able to see the different worlds that various molecules and chemicals created.

As she says, chemistry is everywhere, and it helps us understand the building blocks of life.

And while we may *think* we understand the early solar system or how planets are formed, or what the necessary ingredients are for life to arise, she thinks that we might be wrong about a lot of things. That's why she's like an astrochemistry detective. Instead of doing forensics work on crimes, she's doing forensics work to uncover some of the deepest mysteries of the cosmos.

Ashley has been a research assistant at the Harvard-Smithsonian Center for Astrophysics, using computer models to study the role ice plays in protoplanetary disks. Her research has also taken her to the world-renowned Johns Hopkins University and NASA's Goddard Space Flight Center, where she studied the astrochemistry of Titan using laboratory experiments and computer models. She is now pursuing her PhD in atmospheric sciences at Howard University.

Ashley hopes to one day unlock Titan's secrets and that someday her work will also help find habitable worlds far beyond our own.

> " I HOPE THAT WE SEE MORE CHILDREN FEELING A BIT MORE VISIBLE, FEELING MORE COMFORTABLE ABOUT LOVING SCIENCE AND BEING BLACK. "

# ASTRONOMY IS FOR EVERYONE

Beyond her own research, one of the things most important to Ashley is working to end systemic racism in the fields of science, especially since she has experienced it firsthand. It wasn't always obvious, such as a racial slur; it could be more subtle, such as discouragement to pursue her career, or being made to feel that her work was not as valued as that of someone else who was white. Racism isn't always about words. It's also about actions.

On May 25, 2020, a man named Christian Cooper was walking through Central Park in New York City. Christian, a Black man, was an avid birder. He was in one of his favorite places to bird-watch when he encountered a woman who had her dog off its leash—a clear violation of the rules. He politely asked her to put a leash on the dog, and the woman began to scream at him. She eventually called the police and falsely claimed that Christian was threatening her.

The incident gained a lot of attention on social media, especially in light of the fact that it occurred on the same day as the killing of George Floyd by Minneapolis police.

The Black community was angry and felt that these were perfect examples of how they were being unfairly targeted and didn't feel safe, even while doing harmless things like birding. Black birders, people who either studied birds for a living or simply enjoyed setting out with a pair of binoculars to watch some of our feathered friends, came together and created the hashtag #BlackBirdersWeek in an effort to educate and promote the work Black birders were doing.

Suddenly, Black scientists were banding together to create their own study-specific hashtag. Ashley created #BlackInAstro and co-created #BlackInChem and #BlackInPhysics. To her, it was important not only that people learn about Black people in various scientific fields but also to show the younger generation that they could have a career in science after centuries of being left out.

## RACISM IN SCIENCE

Over the course of history, much of the work done by Black scientists was uncredited—just look at Katherine Johnson—or was claimed by white scientists. While there has been a move to correct such historical wrongs, the question remains: How many more discoveries might have been made if Black people weren't considered to be intellectually inferior and abused throughout history? Black scientists are still underrepresented in the STEM fields, and many of them have asked colleges and universities to make real, systemic change—such as including diverse representation at the highest levels or incorporating historic context in courses—on top of encouraging a younger generation to pursue their dreams.

In addition to giving talks about her research, Ashley speaks about the importance of adding Black voices to the various fields of science. She often says that not many astrochemists look like her. There are so few Black people—especially women—in astronomy and the sciences in general. That, she says, needs to change. She hopes that with the recent #BlackInX movement on social media, more young people will see that they can reach for the stars.

Ashley wants to ensure that Black children know that they can be an astronomer, an ornithologist, a chemist, a paleontologist . . . anything they want to be. She wants academia to ensure that all universities and colleges are inclusive, open spaces for anyone to learn, no matter the color of their skin. But Ashley also wants to see more Black people in decision-making positions so change can come from within.

Her sights are on the future—a future where science is open to anyone. A future where everyone, whether they are Black or Indigenous or Asian or white, can all work together to expand our knowledge of our universe. And she looks forward to the day she and other Black astrochemists will work together on the data collected from Dragonfly and finally understand the chemical processes that might have given rise to life.

# INTO THE GREAT UNKNOWN

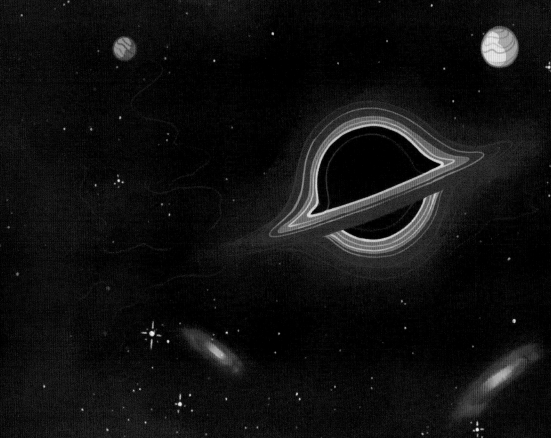

I hope that you enjoyed reading about just some of the work being done by these women, but most importantly, I hope it got you thinking about the universe around us.

There are still so many questions left unanswered, still so much we don't know. What happened on Mars to transform it from a world that may have once boasted an ocean to the arid, rock-strewn planet we know today? What came before the Big Bang? When and how will our universe end? Is there life out there among the stars, or are we all alone? Will we ever find out what dark matter and dark energy are?

But there are so many other things we're just starting to better understand, like black holes, the potential of living on Mars or the moon, and stars that burst with an enormous amount of energy in fractions of a second. Will we ever be able to travel to the edge of our solar system—or to other stars?

I want to know the answers to all of these things, but I know that it takes a lot of research and work and time. For now, I will just have to patiently wait and dream about traveling to other worlds while I follow the awe-inspiring work being done by these extraordinary women.

Their work has just started. Maybe you'd like to pick up the torch?

# PIONEERING WOMEN IN STEM

You've likely heard and seen a lot of the acronym STEM. It stands for science, technology, engineering, and math. These are career streams that have historically been dominated by men. But around the world, from Canada to Brazil to Singapore to India to Australia, there are groups devoted to promoting STEM to young girls. Japan has set a target to have women in 30 percent of the leadership positions in the STEM workforce by 2030. In Kenya, the African Women in Science and Engineering program was launched to help women in STEM. India launched the Indian Girls Code initiative to teach girls to code and make technology more accessible. The world is stepping up!
Read up on these women scientists to learn more about their amazing discoveries and accomplishments.

## MARIA MITCHELL

**1847:** The first woman in the United States to become a professional astronomer. In addition to discovering her own comet, she was a fierce advocate of science education for girls.

## CAROLINE HERSCHEL

**1783:** Discovers an open star cluster. She later discovers nebulae—the clouds of gas and particles that eventually give rise to new stars and planets—and was also the first woman to discover a comet.

## HELEN SAWYER HOGG

**1939:** Publishes a complete catalog of 1,116 variable stars—stars that change in brightness with regularity—in globular clusters, thousands to millions of stars bound by gravity

## DOROTHY VAUGHAN

**1949:** As a mathematician, computer programmer, and the first Black woman supervisor at NACA, she works on one of the most successful satellite launch vehicles in history, the Solid Controlled Orbital Utility Test system, or SCOUT

## ANNIE JUMP CANNON

**1901:** Creates a classification system for stars that is still in use today and uses it to classify more than 225,000 individual stars

## CAROLYN PORCO

**1990:** Becomes the imaging team leader for the Cassini-Huygens mission, bringing the world beautiful images of Saturn and discovering geysers of water vapor on the moon Enceladus. She leads scientists to believe that there is potential for life under its icy crust.

## NANDINI HARINATH

**2014:** The Indian Space Research Organisation successfully achieves Martian orbit, thanks in part to her, the deputy operations director for the Mars Orbiter Mission

## MARGARET BURBIDGE

**1983:** Becomes the president of the American Association for the Advancement of Science. She helps design some of the original instruments for the Hubble Space Telescope.

## KATIE MACK

**2020:** A theoretical astrophysicist, space communicator, and author who studies the big questions about our universe, such as how it came to be, as well as black holes, dark matter, and how our universe might come to an end

## LYNNAE QUICK

**2021:** Awarded the American Astronomical Society's 2021 Harold C. Urey Prize for outstanding achievement in planetary research by an early-career scientist for her work studying cryovolcanism—ice volcanoes—on asteroids

## SOPHIA GAD-NASR

**2018:** As a cosmologist and science communicator, she processes images collected by the Juno mission around Jupiter and studies dark matter, all while bringing greater information about space discoveries to the public

# GLOSSARY

**Aeronautics:** the science of building or flying aircraft

**Analogue:** areas on Earth where conditions are similar to those on other planets or moons

**Artificial satellite:** a human-made object that orbits Earth

**Astrophysicist:** someone who studies stars and other celestial bodies

**Atom:** the smallest unit into which matter can be divided without the release of electrically charged particles

**Big Bang:** the rapid expansion of matter that occurred 13.8 billion years ago giving rise to everything in our universe

**Cosmologist:** someone who studies the universe

**Dark energy:** an unknown, unseen component of space that is causing the rapid expansion of the universe; it is believed that roughly 68 percent of the universe is made up of dark energy

**Dark matter:** an unknown, unseen component of space that makes up roughly 27 percent of the universe; it is only detected through how it interacts with other things around it

**Engineer:** someone who builds and designs machines

**Exoplanet:** a planet outside our solar system that orbits a star other than our sun

**Galaxy:** a system of millions or billions of stars, together with gas and dust, held together by gravity

**Hubble Space Telescope:** a space telescope launched in 1990 in orbit around Earth

**Light-year:** the distance light travels in one Earth year, roughly nine and a half trillion kilometers (or six trillion miles)

**Marsquake:** the shaking of the ground on Mars, similar to earthquakes here on Earth

**Microbial life:** small organisms that are only visible through a microscope

**Molecule:** a group of atoms bonded together

**Nebulae:** clouds of dust and gas in space

**Noctilucent clouds:** rare, high-altitude clouds that are luminous just after sunset or just before sunrise

**Orbital flight:** a flight that completes at least one full turn around a star, planet, or moon

**PhD:** Doctor of Philosophy, the highest academic degree awarded by universities

**SETI:** the search for extraterrestrial intelligence

**Space Age:** a time period when human exploration of space takes place; it is most commonly used to refer to the time between October 4, 1957, when the Soviet Union launched the first human-made satellite, to when humans first visited the moon

**Speed of light:** measured in terms of how long light takes to travel through a vacuum, which is 299,792,458 meters (983,571,056 feet) per second—or 300,000 kilometers (186,000 miles) per second.

**Speed of sound:** varies as sound waves move through different materials; in dry air, the speed of sound is 31.29 meters (70 feet) per second

**Suborbital flight:** a flight where a spacecraft reaches space but does not complete an orbit

**Subsurface ocean:** a large body of water that lies beneath a planet or moon's crust

**TED:** a short form for Technology, Entertainment, Design; an organization that holds talks by influential people and posts free videos to help viewers cultivate a deeper understanding of thousands of different subjects

**Thesis:** a long essay that explains a theory; used in attaining a PhD

**Trajectory:** the path followed by a flying object

**Universe:** all existing matter and space considered as a whole

**U.S.S.R.:** the Union of Soviet Socialist Republics, a former federal socialist state in northern Eurasia that existed from 1922 to 1991; today, the U.S.S.R. is called Russia

**Wavelengths:** the distance between two wave crests in sound or light

# ACKNOWLEDGMENTS

Thank you to Jill Tarter, Tanya Harrison, Emily Lakdawalla, Renée Hložek, Sara Seager, and Ashley Walker for taking time to speak with me. Also, many thanks to everyone at Annick, in particular Kaela Cadieux and Katie Hearn. And thank you to all the women in STEM—those who have come before, and those who continue to forge ahead.

# SOURCES

## BOOKS

Ignotofsky, Rachel. *Women in Science: 50 Fearless Pioneers Who Changed the World*. New York: Ten Speed Press, 2018.

Scoles, Sarah. *Making Contact: Jill Tarter and the Search for Extraterrestrial Intelligence*. New York: Pegasus Books, 2017.

Shetterly, Margot Lee. *Hidden Figures: The American Dream and the Untold Story of the Black Women Mathematicians Who Helped Win the Space Race*. New York: William Morrow, 2016.

## WEBSITES

### KATHERINE JOHNSON

"The Apollo Program." Smithsonian National Air and Space Museum. Accessed May 2, 2022. https://airandspace.si.edu/learn/highlighted-topics-/apollo.

Doody, Dave. "Section 1: Environment, Chapter 4: Trajectories." In *Basics of Space Flight*, 2017 Edition. NASA Science: Solar System Exploration, NASA Jet Propulsion Laboratory. Last updated March 2022. https://solarsystem.nasa.gov/basics/chapter4-1.

Howell, Elizabeth. "Harvard's 'Computers': The Women Who Measured the Stars." Space. com, November 9, 2016. https://www.space.com/34675-harvard-computers.html.

Kois, Dan. "*Hidden Figures'* Heroine Helped Bring Apollo 13 Back to Earth. So Why Isn't She in Apollo 13?" Slate, January 24, 2017. https://slate.com/culture/2017/01/hidden-figures-inspires-a-look-back-at-the-white-faces-of-the-right-stuff-and-apollo-13.html.

Krishna, Swapna, and Kelsey McConnell. "10 Extraordinary Facts About Katherine Johnson, the Late Groundbreaking 'Human Computer.'" *The Portalist*, February 8, 2019. Last updated February 20, 2020. https://theportalist.com/5-extraordinary-facts-about-katherine-johnson.

Lieff Benderly, Beryl. "Presidential Medal of Freedom Honors a NASA 'Computer.'" *Science* (website), December 1, 2015. https://www.science.org/content/article/presidential-medal-freedom-honors-nasa-computer.

Ott, Tim. "Katherine Johnson Biography." Biography.com, October 10, 2016. Last updated January 11, 2021.
https://www.biography.com/scientist/katherine-g-johnson.

Vitug, Eric, ed. "Katherine G. Johnson." NASA, May 24, 2017. Last updated August 6, 2017.
https://www.nasa.gov/feature/katherine-g-johnson.

"West Area Computers." Center for the History of Physics at AIP, summer 2014.
https://www.aip.org/sites/default/files/history/files/AIP-West-Area-Computers-Handout.pdf.

## JILL TARTER

Powell, Corey S. "First Person: Jill Tarter." *American Scientist* 106, no. 5 (September–October 2018): 310.
https://www.americanscientist.org/article/first-person-jill-tarter.

Steele, Bill. "It's the 25th Anniversary of Earth's First Attempt to Phone E.T." *Cornell News*, November 12, 1999.
https://news.cornell.edu/stories/1999/11/25th-anniversary-first-attempt-phone-et-0.

Tarter, Jill. "Are We Alone?" Interview by Ari Stein. 52 Insights, August 17, 2017.
https://www.52-insights.com/jill-tarter-seti-astronomer-are-we-alone-universe-interview-space-science-universe.

Tarter, Jill. "Join the SETI Search." TED Talk, TED2009: The Great Unveiling (conference), February 5, 2009.
https://www.ted.com/talks/jill_tarter_join_the_seti_search.

## EMILY LAKDAWALLA

Emily Lakdawalla (website).
https://www.lakdawalla.com/emily.

"Emily Lakdawalla." The Planetary Society. Accessed May 2, 2022.
https://www.planetary.org/profiles/emily-lakdawalla.

## TANYA HARRISON

Articles by Tanya Harrison, The Planetary Society.
https://www.planetary.org/articles?listauthor=tanya-harrison.

Dr. Tanya Harrison (blog), Medium.
https://tanyaofmars.medium.com.

Harrison, Tanya. "People: Tanya Harrison: Planetary Scientist." Interview by NASA Science: Solar System Exploration, NASA Jet Propulsion Laboratory. Accessed May 2, 2022.
https://solarsystem.nasa.gov/people/2000/tanya-harrison.

Tanya Harrison (website).
https://www.tanyaharrison.com.

"Tanya Harrison Biography." *Ad Astra*. Accessed May 2, 2022.
https://space.nss.org/tanya-harrison-biography.

# SARA SEAGER

Bains, William, Janusz J. Petkowski, Clara Sousa-Silva, and Sara Seager. "New Environmental Model for Thermodynamic Ecology of Biological Phosphine Production." *Science of the Total Environment* 658 (March 2019): 521–536.
https://www.sciencedirect.com/science/article/abs/pii/S004896971834926X.

Boucher, Marc. "Canadian Scientist Sara Seager Has a Gift." SpaceQ, April 19, 2020.
https://spaceq.ca/canadian-scientist-sara-seager-has-a-gift.

Brennan, Pat. "Our Milky Way Galaxy: How Big Is Space?" *Exoplanet Blog: Alien vs. Editor*, NASA Exoplanet Exploration Program, April 2, 2019.
https://exoplanets.nasa.gov/blog/1563/our-milky-way-galaxy-how-big-is-space.

"Exoplanet and Candidate Statistics." NASA Exoplanet Archive, NASA Exoplanet Science Institute, California Institute of Technology. Accessed May 2, 2022.
https://exoplanetarchive.ipac.caltech.edu/docs/counts_detail.html.

The Exoplanet Encylopaedia (catalog).
http://exoplanet.eu/catalog.

Feder, Toni. "Q&A: Sara Seager, Exoplanet Explorer." *Physics Today*, February 27, 2019. Last updated March 1, 2019.
https://physicstoday.scitation.org/do/10.1063/PT.6.4.20190227a/full.

Jenkins, Ann. "A New View of Exoplanets with NASA's Upcoming Webb Telescope." NASA, May 29, 2019.
https://www.nasa.gov/feature/goddard/2019/a-new-view-of-exoplanets-with-nasa-s-webb-telescope.

Jones, Chris. "The Woman Who Might Find Us Another Earth." *New York Times*, December 7, 2016.
https://www.nytimes.com/2016/12/07/magazine/the-world-sees-me-as-the-one-who-will-find-another-earth.html.

Masetti, Maggie. "Why Infrared? (Exoplanet Edition)." *NASA Blueshift* (blog), Astrophysics Science Division, NASA Goddard Space Flight Center, October 24, 2013.
https://asd.gsfc.nasa.gov/blueshift/index.php/2013/10/24/maggies-blog-why-infrared-exoplanet-edition.

McGowen, Kerry. "Atmospheric Gases on Other Planets Could Help Us Find Alien Life." Science in the News blog, Harvard University, July 25, 2020.
http://sitn.hms.harvard.edu/flash/2020/atmospheric-gases-on-other-planets-could-help-us-find-alien-life.

Open Exoplanet Catalogue.
http://www.openexoplanetcatalogue.com.

Rodriguez, Joshua. "Flower Power: NASA Reveals Spring Starshade Animation." NASA/JPL/Caltech. NASA Exoplanet Exploration Program. Last updated September 23, 2020.
https://exoplanets.nasa.gov/resources/1015/flower-power-nasa-reveals-spring-starshade-an-imation.

Sara Seager (website).
https://www.saraseager.com.

Seager, Sara, Janusz J. Petkowski, Peter Gao, William Bains, Noelle C. Bryan, Sukrit Ranjan, and Jane Greaves. "The Venusian Lower Atmosphere Haze as a Depot for Desiccated Microbial Life: A Proposed Life Cycle for Persistence of the Venusian Aerial Biosphere." *Astrobiology* 21, no. 10 (October 2021): 1206–1223.
https://www.liebertpub.com/doi/10.1089/ast.2020.2244.

"The Search for Life." NASA Exoplanet Exploration Program. Last updated April 2, 2021.
https://exoplanets.nasa.gov/search-for-life/habitable-zone.

"Starshades." New Worlds, Center for Astrophysics and Space Astronomy (CASA), University of Colorado, Boulder. Accessed May 2, 2022.
https://newworlds.colorado.edu/starshade.

"Starshade Technology Development." NASA Exoplanet Exploration Program. Last updated August 12, 2021.
https://exoplanets.nasa.gov/exep/technology/starshade.

# RENÉE HLOŽEK

"Biography: Renée Hložek." CIFAR. Accessed May 2, 2022.
https://cifar.ca/bios/renee-hlozek/

Hložek, Renée. "Cosmology: Discovering the Unknown." TED Talk, TEDxSpenceSchool (event), January 28, 2014.
https://www.youtube.com/watch?v=3VhyGjbC3n8.

Hložek, Renée. "The Death of the Universe." Directed by Giant Animation Studios. TED-Ed, December 2013.
https://www.ted.com/talks/renee_hlozek_the_death_of_the_universe.

Hložek, Renée. "Making Sense of Everything We Know about Space." TED Archive, TED2015 Fellows Retreat (conference), August 2015.
https://www.youtube.com/watch?v=JbdcqUUJsCk.

Lemonick, Michael D. "Ride the Science Train—aka the New York Subway." *Time*, October 28, 2013.
https://science.time.com/2013/10/28/ride-the-science-train-aka-the-new-york-subway.

"Prof. Renée Hložek." Dunlap Institute for Astronomy and Astrophysics, University of Toronto. Accessed May 2, 2022.
https://www.dunlap.utoronto.ca/dunlap-people/prof-renee-hlozek.

Renée Hložek's Curriculum Vitae.
https://utoronto.academia.edu/ReneeHlozek/CurriculumVitae.

# ASHLEY WALKER

De los Reyes, Mia. "#BlackInAstro Experiences: Ashley Walker." Astrobites, June 22, 2020.
https://astrobites.org/2020/06/22/black-in-astro-ashley-walker.

Gohd, Chelsea. "Carbon-Rich Alien Planets Could Be Made of Diamonds." Space.com, September 15, 2020.
https://www.space.com/carbon-exoplanets-made-of-diamonds.html.

# INDEX